The Great Mystery of God's Providence,
and Other Works
by George Gifford
with chapters by C. Matthew McMahon

Copyright Information

The Great Mystery of God's Providence, and Other Works by George Gifford, with chapters by C. Matthew McMahon
Edited by Susan Ruth and Therese B. McMahon

Copyright ©2021 by Puritan Publications and A Puritan's Mind

Some language and grammar have been updated from the original manuscript. Any change in wording or punctuation has not changed the intent or meaning of the original author(s), and has been made to aid the modern reader.

Published by Puritan Publications
A Ministry of A Puritan's Mind ®
Crossville, TN
www.puritanpublications.com
www.apuritansmind.com

All rights reserved. No part of this publication may be reproduced, stored in a retrieval system or transmitted in any form by any means, electronic, mechanical, photocopy, recording or otherwise, without the prior permission of the publisher, except as provided by USA copyright law.

Manufactured in the United States of America

eISBN: 978-1-62663-416-9
ISBN: 978-1-62663-417-6

Table of Contents

Introduction 4

Meet George Gifford 8

The Great Mystery of God's Providence 17

A Sermon on James 2 65

A Sermon on James 3 98

A Treatise of True Fortitude 127

A Sermon on Psalm 133 162

A Sermon on the Parable of the Sower 192

Other Helpful Books by George Gifford Published by Puritan Publications 215

Introduction
by C. Matthew McMahon, Ph.D. Th.D.

Among puritan ministers, Gifford does not disappoint as a thorough exegete of God's word, with practical exactness in his preaching, while at the same time, being eminently simple to understand. He is always pastoral in his application, and cared immensely for those listening to him preach the Gospel, and its sundry doctrines. In covering such important areas, Gifford *shines* as a godly preacher and puritan.

This particular work by Gifford is the result of continued labor to bring the Christian church sound teaching from relatively unknown puritans that ought to be known. Most thoughtful ministers and theologians today are in fact very unaware of his writings or his life, and you too, reader, may be unaware of this spiritual giant in Christ's church, who was a beacon light for God's people. Compiled in this volume are six godly works that will place Gifford among the best puritans you can read (you will thoroughly agree with that sentiment upon finishing the first section on God's providence). He is, by careful preaching and writing, one of those master preachers who bring people into the throne room of Jesus Christ to bow before his Kingly majesty.

These works are a *potpourri* of available manuscripts that complete "almost" all of Gifford's works to current modern print. There is one final work, a commentary on Ecclesiastes, that we will take up in the future that will complete the available publishing of all his known pieces by this faithful puritan. But these works are needful for Christ's church, in that they tackle various, but central, biblical truths that enhance the Christian's walk in an effort to glorify the living Christ.

The first work is worth the cost of the volume itself. It is his treatise on *The Great Mystery of God's Providence*. He bases this work on Genesis 45:8, and the historical narrative of Joseph coming to power in Egypt by God's providence. One would think that he considers only providence itself in this most remarkable series of events, but he more particularly deals with the question, "To what degree does the holy and righteous God make use of the evil actions of wicked men and devils, without any impeachment of his righteousness and holiness?" This is a wonderful and masterful treatise that will expand your view of the great mystery of God's providence in the world, not only in Joseph's time, but throughout all of redemptive history, including our own time.

In his second piece, he covers James 2:26, "...so faith without works is dead," while comparing both Paul's use of justification by faith, and James' use of justification by works. This question has been a controversy in many eras of the Christians church, and Gifford rightly and astutely demonstrates that Paul and James are eminently compatible in their views, and explains how this is so.

Introduction

In his third sermon on James 3, he covers the manner in which the Christian's speech ought to glorify God, and how, very often, that it does not. This is especially proven out by dealing with Christians in the church, where out of the same mouth comes blessing and cursing.

In his fourth piece, he demonstrates the need and virtue of true fortitude to the glory of God. In this, he considers the strength and vigor of the Christian in all they do in zeal for the glory of Christ.

In his fifth piece on Psalm 133:1 he covers the need and commendation of unity in the church, the unity of the Spirit, in the bond of peace, as set down by David in the Psalm, and echoed in Ephesians by Paul.

In his last piece is an explanation of the parable of the sower, from Matt. 13:1-9. He teaches that in the innumerable multitude that came to hear Christ's heavenly doctrine, the Savior shows that out of this great number of people that were so zealous and traveled so far, there were three groups out of four that did not profit by his teaching and were therefore still creatures under damnation. Only one group of the four were true hearers.

Gifford is very easy to read, yet, exegetically sound and practically deep. May the Lord bless you as you take time to study along with Gifford on these godly and biblical topics.

In Christ's eternal and gracious power,

The Great Mystery of God's Providence and Other Works

C. Matthew McMahon, Ph.D., Th.D.
From my study, June, 2021

Meet George Gifford
Edited by C. Matthew McMahon, Ph.D., Th.D.

George Gifford (1547-1620) was a most excellent puritan divine educated in Hart-hall, Oxford, where he continued for a number of years. In 1582 he became vicar of Maldon in Essex.[1] The *Oxford Historian* describes him as "a very noted preacher, a man admirably well versed in the various branches of good literature, and a great enemy to popery."[2] Mr. Strype says, "he was a great and diligent preacher, and much esteemed by many people of rank. By his labors he brought the town to much more sobriety and knowledge of true religion."[3] He was a *decided* puritan, and had scrupled conformity in various particulars. He wrote with great zeal against the Brownists, and in defense of the church. But all these things were mere trifles, so long as he did not admire the ceremonies, nor come up to the standard of conformity required by the prelates. Therefore, having preached the doctrine of limited obedience to the civil magistrate, complaints were brought against him, and he was immediately suspended and cast into prison. This was in the year 1584.

About the same time, this learned divine, and twenty-seven other ministers of Essex, presented a supplication to the lords of the council. The ministers

---

[1] Fuller's *Hist. of Cam.* p. 75.
[2] Wilkins on *Preaching*, p. 83.
[3] Palmer's *Noncon. Mem.* vol. ii. p. 38.

who subscribed to this supplication were highly celebrated for learning, piety, and usefulness, many of whom were already suspended for nonconformity. In the supplication they express themselves as follows. "We cheerfully and boldly offer this our humble suit unto your honors, being our only sanctuary upon earth, next to her majesty, to which we can repair in our present necessity. And most of all we are encouraged, when we consider how richly God has adorned your honors with knowledge, wisdom, and zeal for the gospel, and with godly care and tender love to those who profess the same. Most humbly, therefore, we beseech your honors, with your accustomed favor in all godly and just causes, to hear and to judge of our matters. We have received the charge of her majesty's loyal and faithful subjects, to instruct and teach our people in the way of life; and every one of us having this from the God of heaven, *Woe be unto me, if I preach not the gospel*, we have all endeavored to discharge our duties, and to approve ourselves both to God and men. Notwithstanding this, we are in great heaviness, and some of us already put to silence, and the rest living in fear; not that we have been, or can be charged, we hope, with false doctrine, or slanderous life; but because we refuse to subscribe that there is nothing contained in the *Book of Common Prayer* contrary to the word of God.[4] We do protest in the sight of God, who searches all hearts, that we do not refuse from a desire to dissent, or

---

[4] Strype's *Aylmer*, p. 110.

from any sinister affection; soliciting a redress of their thought it does not bear out in the fear of God, and from the necessity of conscience. The apostle teaches, that a person who doubts is "condemned if he eats."[5] If a man then be condemned for doing a lawful action, because he doubts whether it be lawful; how much more should we incur the displeasure of the Lord, and justly deserve his wrath, if we should subscribe, being fully persuaded that there are some things in the book contrary to his word? If our reasons might be so answered by the doctrine of the Bible, and we could be persuaded that we might subscribe lawfully, and in the fear of God, we would willingly consent. In these and other respects we humbly crave your honorable protection, as those who from the heart do entirely love, honor, and obey her excellent majesty and your honors, in the Lord. Giving most hearty thanks to God for all the blessings we have received from him, by your government, constantly praying, night and day, that he will bless and preserve her majesty and your honors to eternal salvation.[6]

> Your honors poor and humble supplicants,
> George Gifford, Samuel Cotesford, Richard Rogers, Richard Illison, Nicholas Colpotts, William Serdge, Lawrance Newman, Edmund Barker, William Dike, Richard Blackwell, Thomas Chaplain, Thomas Howell, Arthur Dent,

---

[5] MS. *Register*, p. 330.
[6] Strype's *Whitgif.* p. 158.

Mark Wirsdale, Thomas Redrich, Robert Edmonds, Giles Whiting, Augustine Pigot, Ralph Hawden, Camiulus Rusticus, Jeffery Jesselin, John Jiuckle, Thomas Upcue, Thomas Carew, Roger Carr, John Bishop, John Wilton."[7]

When Mr. Gilford was brought to trial before the high commission, his enemies utterly failed in their evidence, and he was accordingly released. This, however, was not the end of his troubles. He did not enjoy his liberty for very long. Bishop Aylmer appointed spies to watch him, and fresh complaints were soon brought against him on account of his nonconformity. Again he was suspended and cast into prison.[8] On this he made application to the lord treasurer, who endeavored to obtain the favor of the archbishop; but his grace having consulted his brother of London, told the treasurer that he was a ringleader of the nonconformists; that he himself had received complaints against him, and was determined to bring him before the high commission.[9]

Mr. Gifford had many friends, and was greatly beloved by his numerous hearers. The parishioners of Maldon, therefore, presented a petition to the bishop, in behalf of their minister, signed by fifty-two people, two of whom were bailiffs of the town, two justices of the

---

[7] Neal's *Puritans*, vol. 1, p. 379.
[8] Strype's *Whitgift*, p. 159.
[9] Strype's *Aylmer*, pp. 111-112.

peace, four aldermen, fifteen head burgesses, and other respectable people. In this petition, they showed that his former accusations had been proved to be false; that the present charges were only the slanderous accusations of wicked men, who sought to injure his reputation and usefulness; that they themselves and a great part of the town had derived the greatest benefit from his ministry; that his doctrine was always sound and good; that in all his preaching and catechizing he taught obedience to magistrates; that he used no conventicles; and that his life was modest, discreet, and unreprovable. For these reasons they earnestly entreated his grace in restoring him to his ministry.[10] Indeed, the distresses of the people in Essex were at this time so great, that the inhabitants of Maldon and the surrounding country presented a petition to parliament for the removal of present grievances. In this petition, now before me, they complain, in most affecting language, that nearly all their learned and useful ministers were forbidden to preach, or deprived of their livings; and that ignorant and wicked ministers were put in their places.

These endeavors proved ineffectual. Mr. Gifford did not enjoy his liberty for several years, as appears from a supplication of several of the suspended ministers in Essex, presented to parliament, dated March 8, 1587, when he was still under the episcopal censure. It will be proper to give the substance of it in their own words. "In most humble and reverent duty to this high and

---

[10] *MS. Register*, p. 748.

honorable court of parliament, sundry of the ministers and preachers of God's holy word in the county of Essex, present this our earnest supplication, and lamentable complaint, beseeching you upon our knees for the Lord's sake, and the sake of his people, whose salvation it concerns, to bow down a gracious ear to this our most dutiful suit, and to take such order as to your godly wisdom shall be thought most convenient. Your humble suppliants having, by the goodness of God, conducted themselves at all times, both in their doctrine and life, as becomes their vocation, they submit themselves to any trial and punishment, if it should be found otherwise. Notwithstanding this, they have been a long time, and still are, grievously troubled and molested; of which troubles this is one of the heaviest, that we are hindered from the service of God in our public ministry. To this restraint we have hitherto yielded and kept silence."

He continues, "We hoped, from the equity of our cause, the means that have been used, and the necessities of our people, that our suspension would have been taken off by those whose censure lieth upon us. But they neither restored us to our ministry, nor furnished the people with suitable persons to suitors to them, desiring him we might be restored to our former service and usefulness among them; and, notwithstanding our cause has been recommended to them by some of the chief nobility in the land, even of her majesty in her honorable privy council, we have obtained no relief for ourselves, nor comfort for our distressed people. Therefore, to appear before this high and honorable court of parliament, is the only means left to us; that if there be in us no desert of so heavy a sentence, it may please this high court to take such order for the relief of your most humble suppliants as to your godly wisdom shall be thought convenient."

"We, indeed, acknowledge that diverse causes of our restraint are alleged against us; but our earnest desire is, that this high court would by some means be informed of this weighty matter. The chief of them is our refusing to subscribe to certain articles relating to the present policy of the church, that every word and ceremony appointed to be read and used in the *Book of Common Prayer*, is according to the word of God. We declared that we could not, with a good conscience, subscribe to all that was required of us; and we humbly requested to have our doubts removed, and to be satisfied in the things required; but we have not received one word of answer to this day; and their former rigorous proceedings have not in the least been mitigated."

"We humbly pray this high court to be assured of our dutiful obedience to all lawful authority, unto which, as we and our people have been humbled by the ordinance of God, and for conscience sake, with all our hearts, we promise and protest our submission. We seek unto you to obtain some relief for us. And we commit our lives and whole estate to Almighty God, to your gracious clemency, and to the care of her right excellent majesty, ceasing not, day and night, to pray that the blessings of grace and glory may rest upon you forever."

This supplication was signed by George Gifford, Ralph Hawden, William Tunstall, John Huckle, Giles Whiting, and Roger Carr; but whether it proved of any advantage, is extremely doubtful. Most probably they continued much longer under suspension. He lived to a good old age, and died about the year 1620.

His works (which Puritan Publications is currently working to republish) are:
1. Country Divinity, containing a Discourse of certain points of Religion among the Common sort of Christians, with a plain Confutation thereof, 1581.
2. A Sermon on the Parable of the Sower, 1581.
3. A Dialogue between a Papist and a Protestant, applied to the capacity of the Unlearned, 1583.
4. Against the Priesthood and sacrifice of the Church of Rome, in which you may perceive their Impiety in usurping that Office and Action which ever appertained to Christ only, 1584.
5. A Sermon on 2 Peter 1:11, 1584.
6. A Catechism, giving a most excellent light to those that seek to enter the Path-way to Salvation, 1580.
7. A Sermon on James 2:14-26, 1586.
8. A Discourse of the subtle Practices of Devils by Witches and Sorcerers, 1587.
9. Sermons on the first four Chapters and part of the fifth chapter of Ecclesiastes, 1589.

10. A short Treatise against the Donatists of England, whom we call Brownists, in which, by Answer unto their Writings, their Heresies are noted, 1590.

11. A Plain Declaration that our Brownists be full Donatists, by comparing them together from point to point out of the writings of Augustine, 1591.

12. A Reply to Mr. Job. Greenwood and Hen. Barrow, touching on Prayer, in which their gross Ignorance is detected, 1591.

13. A Sermon at Paul's Cross, on Psalm 133, 1591.

14. A Dialogue concerning Witches and Witchcrafts; in which is laid open how craftily the Devil deceiveth not only the Witches, but others, 1593.

15. A Treatise of True Fortitude, 1594.

16. A Commentary or Sermons on the whole Book of Revelation, 1596.

17. Two Sermons on 1 Peter 5:8-9, 1598.

18. Four Sermons upon several parts of Scripture, 1598.

19. An Exposition on the Song of Solomon, 1612.

20. Five Sermons on the Song of Solomon, 1620.

21. An English Translation of Dr. Fulke's Prelections on the Holy Revelations.

The Great Mystery of God's Providence[11]

TO THE READER.

Next to the knowledge and belief of one God and the essentials of religion, there is no greater truth more needed by all people than this topic before us, namely, to what degree the holy and righteous God makes use of the evil actions of wicked men and devils, without any impeachment of his righteousness and holiness. To think that this makes him the author or approver of sin shows the gross ignorance and misunderstanding which, in all ages, has promoted atheism and irreligion among the wicked of this world who say in their hearts there is no God, or he is not a righteous and holy God. And the prosperity of wicked men in their evil actions, along with the suffering of good men, have caused many to stumble. The truth of this matter lies in the middle, between the two extremes. And if the reader brings a serious mind to know the truth, I know he will find this matter so plainly, though briefly stated and determined,

---

[11] *The Great Mystery of Providence or, The various Methods of God in Ordering and Overruling the Actions of Wicked Men and Devils to great and glorious Purposes. With the Vindication of his Holiness therein.* BEING The Substance of several sermons preached by the Reverend, Judicious, and Orthodox Divine Mr. George Gifford, Late Minister of St. Dunstan in the East, London. Heb. 11:4, "He being dead, yet speaketh." (London: Printed for S. Crouch, at the Corner of Pope's-head Alley near the Royal Exchange in Cornhill, 1695).

as to answer all material objections from atheists and those who profanely deny this truth, being wise in their own conceit. If such men, instead of murmuring and fretting, will give consideration to these truths, they will come to adore that infinite wisdom and goodness that can bring good out of evil and overrule all the sins and follies of men, to the greater manifestation of his own glorious attributes and the good welfare of his church.

The reader must expect nothing more than the Apostle Paul's great plainness of speech, which best becomes divinity, and especially regarding the weighty subject before us. Therefore I will conclude with only one request to the reader, that he consider these lines with the same spirit which the author declares he had in their delivery, namely, with a holy fear and trembling, and then I have no doubt that he will receive that benefit and advantage by them as will give abundant cause to bless God for them, which is the chief end of the publisher.

J.D.

"So now it was not you that sent me hither, but God: and he has made me a father to Pharaoh, and Lord of all his house, and a ruler throughout all the land of Egypt," (Gen. 45:8).

I have previously spoken of the joyful discovery of Joseph to his brothers from this chapter, after his rough treating of them. After so many fears and dangers, the sun finally breaks through the clouds and he cries out to them, "I am Joseph." In this narrative is an emblem of how God deals with his own people. He leads them at first into crooked paths, but then, after all these tempests and storms, he brings joy and peace at last. And I proposed to you, how that after some great affliction and seeming spiritual desertion when God appears to show himself as an enemy to his people, at last he shines forth and says, "I am your God and Savior."

The second thing I have previously considered from this passage is Joseph's pardoning and loving his brothers that had so barbarously sold him into slavery. He is now so far from revenging himself of them that he loves and embraces them. Here we have a most worthy example of that high and excellent duty of loving and forgiving those that injure us, and to understand that the true and noblest way of revenging injuries is by overcoming evil with good.

I come now to the next thing, and that is the arguments Joseph uses to comfort his brothers that were so overcome with shame and fear. He repeats this three times. First, he praises the providence of God in working this great thing, "It was not you that sent me hither, but God." It is true that you sold me. But look to the good hand and providence of God in it. God sent me before you; it was not you that sent me here, but God.

This is to raise them, as well as us, up to a serious contemplation of how all the evils of men are ordered by the wise providence of God to good purposes. In this action God and they worked together. They sold Joseph, and God sent him for good, for the preservation of God's people in Jacob's family. In this way, *we look at the providence of God in overruling the actions of wicked men.*

First, see how often Joseph acknowledges the hand and providence of God in this matter. I believe nothing will make us more willing to forgive those who have done us harm than to recognize the providence of God, and trust everything to that instead of looking at instruments and second causes without considering the hand of God in them.

Secondly, he says, "God sent me before you, to preserve you a posterity, and to save your lives by a great deliverance; and it was not you that sent me hither, but God." I observe here God's gracious providence and care over his church and children. This is one of the most excellent observations of God's providence towards his children in the whole Scripture. When God intended to bring a most dreadful famine upon the world, in which Jacob and his family would probably have perished, he made provision for him and them 20 years beforehand, in such a way as Jacob and Joseph would have never thought of. Twenty years beforehand, he sent Joseph to be a harbinger for his church and people. In a secret and infallible manner God orders all events that, at last, tend to the good of his church.

Here we find several cross providences in this history of Joseph and his brothers, and yet they all contribute to this good end and conclusion. This should teach us that in all the difficulties and troubles that beset God's church, when we do not know what will become of us, we can rely on the providence of God to provide for us in ways and through means that we have no idea of.

Thirdly, I will consider the providence of God in governing and overruling the actions of wicked men. "It was not you that sent me here, but God," and yet certainly, they had a hand in the action. It was God that overruled their counsels; all the actions of sinful men, yes, of the devils themselves, are ordered by a strange but most wise counsel of God himself. It is a point of great concern to resolve how the righteousness and holiness of God can consist in ordering and ruling the sins of mankind. There is a great difference among those who desire to reconcile the providence of God in the actions of sinful men with his holiness, justice, and the liberty and freedom of mankind.

First, I will demonstrate from this example that all the actions of men, even their sinful actions, are under the providence of God; they sold Joseph, and God sent him.

Secondly, I will consider the efficiency or concurrence God has with the actions of ungodly men.

Thirdly, I will consider how God works, and how he ordains the actions of wicked men to ends beyond what they desired or designed. This is a point to be weighed and considered in regard to our present fears.

Let us begin with the actions of men and devils, both good and bad. All the sins of wicked men and devils are under the government of the providence of God. (1.) I will prove this point with four or five places in Scripture, and the first will be drawn from those general places in Scripture that ascribe everything to the will and providence of God as does Psalm 35:6, "Whatever the Lord pleased, that did he in heaven and in earth." Nothing comes to pass without the will of God (Dan. 4:35). He does according to his will with all the armies of heaven and earth, and none can stay his hand.

It is true that many things are contrary to the preceptive part of God's will, but nothing comes to pass without the providence of God, or against what he would have done. Even the devils themselves, when they cross the preceptive will of God, they then most fulfill the will of his providence. "There are many devices in a man's heart; nevertheless the counsel of the LORD, that shall stand," (Prov. 19:21). Whatever designs men or devils may have, he tells us they all act according to the providential will of God.

(2.) Actions done by wicked men are said to be done by the eternal counsel and ordination of God and are the contrivance of God's decrees: it was so in this case of Joseph. God had decreed Joseph's advancement in Egypt, yet this was not brought to pass without the sin of his brothers.

I will give you one instance in Scripture that proved to be the greatest blessing to mankind of any in the world, yet was brought to pass by the greatest villainy that ever was in the world, which is the suffering of our blessed Lord and Savior. Acts 2:23 says, "Him, being delivered by the determinate counsel and foreknowledge of God, you have taken, and by wicked hands crucified and slain." In the same action there was the wickedness and envy of the scribes and pharisees and the villainy and treachery of Judas' betrayal. And yet all this was done by the determinate counsel and foreknowledge of God. Acts 4:27-28 states, "For of a truth against thy holy child Jesus, both Herod and Pontius Pilate, and the Gentiles and people of Israel were gathered together for to do whatsoever thy hand and thy counsel determined before to be done." This is a singular comfort, that all things come to pass not according to wicked men's counsels, but according to what God determines.

(3.) Even when wicked men are said to do the most unjust actions, they are still the instruments of

God's providence, to execute his counsels, his designs, and his purposes. In Isaiah 10:5, God's church was about to be invaded by the Assyrians, "O Assyrian, the rod of mine anger, and the staff in their hand is mine indignation; I will send him against a hypocritical nation. Howbeit he meaneth not so, neither does he think so, but it is in his heart to destroy and cut off nations." That is, this proud prince thinks nothing of God's providence and purposes in this matter. His design is to gratify his pride, revenge, and covetousness. But God almighty gives way to it for other holy and wise ends. And again, verse 15 says, "Shall the axe boast itself against him that heweth therewith? Or will the saw magnify itself against him that shaketh it? As if the rod should shake itself against them that lift it up, or as if the staff should lift up itself, if it were no wood." There is a great emphasis in these words to show that wicked men and their actions are all in the hands of God, as the ax and the saw in the hand of the workman.

(4.) Even when wicked men go about wicked actions, God is said to stir them up to it: so, in this instance of Joseph, and in that of Isaiah 10:6, God sends the Assyrians against a hypocritical nation to punish and chastise them. Likewise, in 2 Samuel 12:11, you see there that God threatens to raise up evil against David in his own house, by the rebellion of his son Absalom with his villainy and insolence against his father's wives and concubines. Was God the cause of this wickedness in Absalom? No, but as Absalom had these lusts within himself, God permitted him to exercise them for the punishment of David's sin. 2 Samuel 16:11 says, "Shimei does unjustly revile David, but the Lord has sent Shimei to curse David and to punish David for his former sins." Psalm 105:25 says, "He turned the hearts of the Egyptians to hate his people, and to deal subtly with his servants." He made use of their sin for righteous ends.

(5.) I observe in Scripture that the children of God, whenever they suffered most unjustly from wicked men, have not attributed it so much to the instruments as to the justice of God. For example, I give you here an instance with Joseph, "It was not you that sent me hither, but God." Also, in Job you can see what a complication of wickedness there was to bring about his afflictions, there was the devil's malice seeking to ruin and destroy him. There was also the malice of wicked men, the Chaldeans and Sabeans, and yet in Job 1:21, he ascribes all to the providence of God, "The Lord giveth, and the Lord taketh away, blessed be the name of the Lord." So, David, when his son Absalom rebelled against him, still he cries, "it is the Lord." And in the book of the Lamentations, when Israel had been so barbarously destroyed by their enemies, they referred all to the providence of God. And in that act of betrayal and murdering of our Savior, there was an immeasurable amount of wickedness in men. Yet our blessed Savior expressly said it was the cup that his heavenly Father gave him to drink.

Therefore, in all unjust oppressions, it is our work and duty to look above men to the providence of God. We must hear the *voice* of the rod, as well as him who appointed it, and not dwell too much on the instruments or second causes for they are just the ax or the staff or the rod. It is God's hand that limits, orders, and appoints them for holy and gracious ends. And so much for the first part, how that all the actions of wicked men are ordered by the will and providence of God.

Secondly, I come now to inquire how far the holy and righteous God can or does concur in the evil actions of men. That he does so is most certain. But how far, is the question, and most interpreters have been puzzled in this matter. Thus, I will undertake to do it first negatively, for I will tell you the truth lies between two extremes: (1.) It is the highest blasphemy for any to charge God with being the author of sin. (2.) But there is another extreme to be avoided, which is to think this providence of God is only a bare permission of sin. Afterwards I will show you more particularly of the influence and concurrence of the most holy, wise, and good God in the evil actions of wicked men.

First, almighty God is not, neither can he be, the author or proper cause of any sin. Let this be established as truth, that he never works sin itself, or moves us to sin inwardly. He does not move men to sin, because from these conclusions some adversaries would charge sin to God. God can neither do sin nor compel us to sin; to affirm this would be very blasphemy for, first, God is the supreme good, he is all goodness, holiness, and light, and there can be no evil or darkness in him. So, to ascribe evil and sin to the Supreme Good is to make light the cause of darkness. Hebrews 6:18 says, "It is impossible for God to lie." Again, it is impossible for him who hates sin, who forbids it and severely punishes it, to be its author. It would be the most unjust thing in the world for God to punish that which he himself causes. Again I consider, if God should do so, sin would not be sin, for all sin is that which is contrary to God's will and law; and therefore the apostle James tells us, "let no man say when he is tempted that he is tempted of God, for God cannot be tempted, nether tempteth he any man," (James 1:13). It is inconsistent with the holiness and purity of God to be in any form the author of sin; therefore, Basil said that it is as high a blasphemy to make God the author of sin as it is to deny him to be God. No, beloved, all sin comes from the creature. "Thy destruction is of thyself," though God makes use of it for gracious purposes. For example, the envy and malice of Joseph's brothers came from them, but God ordered it for the good of his people. We must distinguish between the *cause* of sin and the *use* of sin; man is the cause of sin and the actor of sin, but God can use sin for purposes beyond what man designed by it. You know the viper has poison in it, which is of a destructive nature, and yet a skillful physician can make use of this poison as an antidote against poison.

I will draw this as a second caution, that in God's ordering and making use of sin there is more than his bare permission of sin, that is, to let men be wicked, and take no further care in it. No, I say, in all those places I have quoted, God sending Joseph into Egypt, *etc.*, there is divine purpose and efficiency. Most of the sins that are done in the world are done by evil men, and though God is not the author, he is the Orderer, the Governor, and the Disposer of them. A wise king can make use of a traitor to bring to pass his own ends, so God makes use of wicked men's sins to work contrary to their ends. Joseph's brothers never thought of bringing about God's end in their malice against him; they only desired to satisfy their own lust. So, God makes use of wicked men's covetousness and ambition to chastise his people and to do them good.

Section 2

I will now consider this next point, though I must tell you that I do so with as much fear and trembling as I have ever had on any subject: namely, how far the holy and wise God does and may enter into the evil actions of sinful men. Using the Scriptures, I will break this down into nine points.

1. God concurs by permitting them or not hindering the committing of those sins as he might have done. This is expressed in Acts 14:16, "He allowed them to walk in their own ways," the apostle said. It is very clear so far that no sin in the world could be done if God

did not permit it. And I will show you several ways in which God hinders the commission of sin. For example, he hindered Abimelech from committing sin with Abraham's wife (Gen. 20:6). He hindered Balaam when he came with a resolution to curse Israel. He hindered Esau from hurting his brother Jacob. The devils in hell are under chains. God can hinder them, and does hinder them, when he will. For example, Satan could not touch Job nor his cattle until God gave him liberty. There are several ways and means whereby God does this: (1.) By taking away the power of wicked men, as he did with Jeroboam when he put forth his hand against the prophet. Sometimes he stirs up another power to deliver his people from oppression by secretly inclining the hearts of men to do good to those they had planned to hurt, as he did with Laban when he went after Jacob. God sent Abigail to divert David from exercising his intended revenge against Nabal. When God removes these impediments, it is the first way God concurs. We are much obliged to God for keeping wicked men and devils in bonds and for limiting their malice and enmity, for if God gave leave to them to execute their power and malice, all the world would quickly be in flames.

2. God concurs in the evil actions of men by a general cooperation in the action itself, for you must know God almighty has an immediate influence and concourse in all the actions of his creatures, both good and bad. Acts 17:28 states, "In him we live and move and have our being." All Christians and most philosophers

agree that all actions of the creature depend on the motion and influence of the first cause. I will say to those that curse and swear and blaspheme the name of God, they could not move their tongues if God did not give them leave and cooperate in the action. The power with which a thief steals is from God. Nevertheless, God is not the cause of their sin in a moral sense, only in a physical sense. God concurs as to the natural action itself, but not to the sinfulness in that action. God concurs with the natural action, but the responsibility for it proceeds from the wickedness of the sinner's will.

3. God concurs by his providence, in administering occasions and opportunities which wicked men abuse to commit sin. God puts people and circumstances that are not sinful in themselves in the way of sinners, as when he gives wicked men health, strength, wealth, prosperity, beauty, *etc.* These have no harm in themselves, but sinful men often abuse them to satisfy their lusts. These are things that in their own nature would tend to make them better, yet they take occasion to make themselves worse by them. As an example, how often does good admonition make some men worse? The very divinity and miracles of Christ hardened the pharisees' hearts. By his providence God sometimes allows men to fall into wicked company, as he did with Joseph. When his brothers planned to murder him, God ordered some Midianites to go by, that they might sell him to them instead.

4. The fourth way God concurs is by withdrawing his grace and leaving men to the power of their lusts. Wicked men have a violent inclination to many sins, which God in his providence often restrains like a dog that is chained up and cannot do the mischief he has a mind to. But also, sometimes God says, as he did to Ephraim when he was joined himself to idols, "let him alone," (Hosea 4:17). When God leaves men to their sin without any afflictions or terrors of conscience, it is the most dreadful judgment in the world. And by this you may understand those Scriptures where God is said to blind and harden sinners' hearts. This is a most righteous and just act that God does for those who despise his grace and willfully run to sin, that God should punish them with their own sins. When God says, "he that is filthy let him be filthy still," (Rev. 22:11), this is the most dreadful judgment in the world, for when this happens God has given men over to their own lusts.

5. The fifth way is when God leaves sinners to the temptations of the devil or wicked men to tempt and flatter them in their sins. I will give you two or three instances in Scripture. In the first, God permitted a lying spirit to go forth in the nation of the Israelites. God said, "Go, and you will prevail," (Ezek. 14). God tells them that because of the sins of the people he would leave them and allow wicked and false prophets to deceive them, (2 Thess. 2). The coming and prevailing of *antichrist* will include a mass deception of unrighteousness

with all power, and signs, and lying wonders. Why does God allow false prophets to work signs and wonders? Because people do not receive the truth that they might be saved, so God gives them over to strong delusions, to believe lies, that they may be damned. God has also sent forth a lying spirit in our day, by which our adversaries have drawn away thousands. And what is the reason? Because they have rejected the light of the gospel. Popery persuades people to act unnatural to parents and to destroy cities and kingdoms, as the apostle says in 2 Timothy 2:16. Such are taken captive of the devil at his will, that is, whatever sin the devil gives them opportunity to commit, they are ready to act on it, and like Judas, give in to the full possession of Satan.

6. A sixth way God's providence in sinful actions is demonstrated (and I desire you to take notice of it) is how he directs the sinner to such and such a particular object, which perhaps he was indifferent to before. For example, a wicked man may be covetous, or angry, or cruel. He may be indifferent to which of these sins he commits, but God in his secret providence moves him to choose one over another. Like a great mastiff in chains, he is indifferent to who he bites and hurts if he is loosed, but the owner lets him loose on the one that he would have him hurt. This is why Solomon tells us that a man devises his own way, but the Lord directs his steps (Prov. 16:9). Nebuchadnezzar, the great king of Babylon, was resolved to attack some of his neighbors. He did not know if it would be Amon or Judea, but God in his

providence directed him to attack Judea (1 Chron. 5:26). God stirred up the spirit of Saul to persecute Christians, and this was done without any sin attributed to God. Scripture says the hearts of kings are in the hand of the Lord, and he turns them as the rivers of water. As those countries where there is little rain from heaven and they must water their gardens with pools, directing the water with gutters which they run where they choose, so God orders the hearts of kings as it best pleases him.

7. A seventh way is when God gives wicked men power and success to prosper in unjust actions. This is constantly verified in Scripture, as well as by experience in the world, that God may allow good people to be afflicted and suffer injustice while wicked men prosper and bring wicked and unjust actions to pass. So, when God raises up a great king to be a scourge to his neighbors, he will give him wisdom, policy, and success; and when the Lord is resolved to punish a nation, he takes away their wisdom and success. This is why God often allows the wicked to prosper and good men for good causes to fall into the hands of wicked and unreasonable men. Christ himself said that the power Pilate had to crucify him was given him from God. You might wonder whether this compromises God's holiness. I answer no, for God does not give wicked men success as a reward for their actions, but to make use of them as the instruments of his providence, no more than if a king uses wicked man to be his hangman, this does not reflect upon the goodness of the king.

8. The eighth way God's providence governs wicked men and their actions (and I desire you to take notice of it) is by limiting, governing, and disposing of wicked men and their actions so that they are not able to hurt whoever they will, nor when they will, but only as far as God would have it. This is what happened with Joseph's brothers. Their plan was to murder him, but: (1.) God stirred up Rueben to divert that purpose. And then, afterward, God brings his ends to pass when he allows them to sell him, and at that very moment orders the Midianites to come by. How admirably this matter was ordered and limited by God! So it was with the Jews who desired to arrest Christ on many occasions, but they could not, because God was not yet ready. However, afterward he tells them, "I taught daily in the temple, and you laid no hands on me, but now is your hour," (Luke 22:53). So, we see how God sometimes stops evil and mischief, and at other times allows it to break out with irresistible violence. Also, as it relates to the continuance of wicked men in their actions, Scripture says the rod of the wicked will not always rest upon the lot of the righteous. It may come upon them, but it will not remain on them, as God will not allow good men to be tempted above what they are able to bear, and wicked men will not be able to put one drop into the cup of bitterness of his saints more than what God has appointed. Indeed, this is the foundation of all our comfort, to remember that whatever we may suffer, wicked men are nothing more than an ax in God's hand.

They cannot, as to time, or continuance, or degrees, go beyond what God has purposed.

9. The last way is by God's overruling and ordering the effects of sin beyond, and many times contrary to, the purpose and design of sinners. This makes up the complete government of sin. It is for you as it was in Joseph's case, you thought it was for evil, but God meant it for good, to bring to pass as it is at this day and to save much people alive. Indeed, beloved, in one and the same action different ends can be proposed. Often wicked men design nothing except to bring about their own malice, covetousness, and envy, but God turns it to many wise and holy ends. So in Job's case, the devil's design was to make him curse and blaspheme God, but God's design was to make Job bless him. God sent Assyria against Israel to punish a hypocritical nation, but his design was not to root up and destroy his own people. Assyria's design was to plunder and destroy, but God's design was to correct sin. So it was in the sufferings of our blessed Savior, the pharisees out of envy sought to murder him, Pilate for fear of his own purposes condemned him, and the soldiers were only interested in their profit. But through all the envy and malice and covetousness, God overruled to bring to pass the greatest blessing that ever befell mankind – the death and resurrection of Christ. Here is the best example to show how God can make wicked men work his ends when they seem most to cross them. Physicians can make an antidote to expel poison out of poison itself.

And I conclude this point in telling you, that the most excellent works of God's providence that were ever brought to pass in the world are those times when he makes use of the sinful actions of men to effect matters quite contrary to what they intended. Herein I have endeavored to clear the providence of God from any mistake of injustice or unholiness, and to show how the holy and wise God overrules and governs the evil actions of wicked men and devils.

SECTION 3

I come now to the third point, and that is, that God almighty can make good use of the sinful actions of wicked men, so that what they intend for evil, he can and often does turn to good. This is here expressed in the text, "God sent me before you to preserve life," and in Genesis 50:20, "As for you, you thought evil against me, but God meant it for good." You will observe in this narrative that the plan of his brothers in sending him away was nothing but the gratifying of their own envy and malice. The Ishmaelites bought him for their own profit. Potiphar's wife cared about nothing but her own lust, and yet all these things were overruled by God almighty for the good of his church. God almighty turns the sins of wicked men to good; he makes them serve his designs for good. I will here vindicate the providence of God from the great quarrel that has been against it in all ages over the actions of wicked men and the great wickedness that is in the world. One thing the atheists say to support their purposes is that if the world is governed by a God so just, holy, and wise, why is there so much wickedness in it? Can he not prevent it? I will show you that God's permitting so much sin in the world is a fruit of his infinite goodness, because he can bring so much good out of it. Augustine said, "God who is infinitely good and powerful, would not permit sin in the world if he were not able to make that sin turn to some great good." All wicked men and devils are under God's dominion. He overrules all their actions, and there is no evil in second causes except where he makes it serve his own holy and wise ends. It is true that sin, as it is in the creature, is the greatest deformity, darkness, and disorder in the world. But God almighty is able to order it as a wise physician can make use of poison to expel poison. So, though sin in itself is so evil, wholly evil, yet God almighty can make it serve his best and wisest ends. For the truth of this proposition, observe that the greatest actions God ever brought to pass in the world have been occasioned by the sins of wicked men. The occasion of sending Christ to pay for the sin of Adam and to bring to pass our redemption could not be done without the concurrence of wicked actions, as Acts 2:23 says, "By wicked hands you have crucified and slain him," and Acts 4:27 says, "For of a truth against thy holy child Jesus, whom thou hast anointed, both Herod, and Pontius Pilate, with the Gentiles, and the people of Israel, were gathered together." Consider how much wickedness there was in that act: the treachery of Judas, the envy of the pharisees, the covetousness of the soldiers, the cruelty of the rest, and yet all this God made use of to bring to pass the most glorious action that ever occurred in the world. I will give you some more instances of this where I may also demonstrate that God makes use of the sins of wicked men for good purposes": (1.) for the manifestation of his own glory, and (2.) to accomplish the great good he does in the world. Romans 3:7 says, "The truth of God abounds by my lie unto his glory, and he makes the wrath of men to praise him." I will mention five attributes of God that are especially illustrated by God's permitting and ordering the sins of wicked men: (1.) The attribute of God's patience and longsuffering. He proclaims himself, "The Lord God, merciful and longsuffering." Where could there have been room for the exercise of his patience and longsuffering if there were no sin? Romans 9:22 says, "How should we know God's patience, if with much longsuffering he did not endure the vessels of wrath fitted to destruction." (2.) The glory of his justice: God's punishing of sinners could not have been done without the permission of sin. "I will get myself glory over Pharaoh." How so? "By executing my judgments upon him for sin; for this cause have I raised thee up, that I may show forth my power in thee, and make known my glory in all the earth." And there is no question, the glory of God is shown forth in the manifestation of his wrath, both here and hereafter. (3.) The glory of his mercy and free grace appear when God pardons sin; how could that have been done if there had been no sin? Romans 5:20 states, "Where sin abounded grace did much more abound." In a word, all the riches of God's mercy and goodness and free grace to the creature presupposes sin. It could not be without sin. Had man remained without sin, Christ would have never died and there would have been no covenant of grace. (4.) The glory of God's admirable wisdom appears in ordering and governing the sins of the world; the chief part of his wisdom consists in bringing to pass those ends by means that seem most improbable and unlikely. As it is in matters of state policy, it is the greatest part of wisdom to know how to govern evil and discontented subjects. There is nothing in the world so contrary to the glory of God as sin; there is nothing that God hates more. Is this not the glory of his wisdom, then, to make wicked men and devils themselves, when they try most to oppose his glory, end up doing him the most honor? I will give you several instances in Scripture where this happened. It happened with Pharaoh and his wicked men when they planned to ruin his people, God turned it to their advantage. Nazianzen said that the masterpiece of God's wisdom is to make enemies do his own work. Lastly, it demonstrates the greatness of his power. The greatness of his power appears in working without means, or contrary to means as when God created the world. Yet there seems to be a greater power in turning evil to good than in making the world because of all there is to oppose it. The almighty power of God brings light out of darkness, evil out of good, and the greatest good out of the greatest evil.

The second general point is this: to show the good that God works in the world by wicked men. (1.) God makes use of wicked men sometimes as the instruments of his vengeance to punish other wicked men. Sometimes he uses evil angels, but especially evil men, to destroy his enemies. He allows one wicked man to execute his justice on another, and he raises up princes and rulers to be instruments of his vengeance upon a wicked nation. In this way God raised up Nebuchadnezzar to punish Israel when they had sinned, though he had no intention at all of serving God's ends, caring only for his own ambition. Yet he was God's instrument. Many times we are frustrated at God's providence when we see wicked rulers conquer and destroy and invade when they have no just right, but we do not consider that they are directed by a higher hand. Sometimes God does it by private men, sometimes he raises up one oppressor to punish another oppressor. Sometimes he raises up rebellious children to punish parents who were disobedient when they were children. Sometimes he punishes with treachery and unfaithfulness those who have been treacherous and unfaithful themselves.

(2.) God makes use of the sins of wicked men to chastise and punish his own people when they have offended and sinned against him. God makes the sins of wicked men as rods to chastise them and bring them back from their wanderings. I will give you one or two famous instances of this from Scripture: Isaiah 10:5-12, "O Assyrian, the rod of my anger, the staff in their hand is my indignation." God tells us he had a job for the king of Assyria, namely, to punish a hypocritical nation, though the king's own desire was to kill and destroy. Another instance is in 2 Samuel 12. You know that David had sinned a great sin, an indelible sin, that God always remembered. Though God pardoned him, he told him he would raise up a sword out of his own bowels to correct him. First, his oldest son Amnon incestuously ravishes his own sister, then Absalom murders Amnon for what he did. Then God uses one of David's top advisors to persuade Absalom to lay with David's wives and concubines when he was away from the city. And finally, this same son organizes a revolt against David before being tragically killed in battle. How many sins were committed in all these matters, and yet God made use of all this to chastise David and bring him to repentance. What follows is an example to illustrate this from a leach's drawing of blood. The physician applies them, and they draw blood to satisfy their natural inclination. But the physician uses them to draw away illness and disease. So wicked men afflict God's people from the hatred they bear them, but God designs it to correct and humble them and to bring them to repentance.

(3.) God makes use of the sins of wicked men for the trial of the graces of his own children; and this is another admirable end, to use the sins of wicked men to make good men better. This occurs in the famous story of Job, when the devil out of malice tempts him to curse God, but God makes use of it to increase Job's graces. I will give you two more examples: (1.) God allows false prophets, seducers, and heretics to go about undermining the true religion in a nation, which is a very sad providence. Yet God has his ends in it, to try his own children and make them more steadfast in the truth. (See Deut. 13.) The Lord tells them that he permits false prophets to come among them, giving signs and wonders which may come to pass in order to "prove thee, and to know whether thou wilt love the Lord thy God with all thy heart, and with all thy soul." This is also expressed in 1 Corinthians 11:19 where the apostle tells them there must be heresies, "so that they which are approved may be made manifest." God allows seducers to come into a church in order to better establish good men in the truths they have received. Ignorant and unstable men are quickly drawn aside to errors, but when true religion is shaken by errors and heresies, there is nothing that makes good men examine diligently the truths of religion and to conform themselves more carefully to them than this. So, the wicked practices and lives of some make those that are good men more diligent, more watchful, and more exact in their conversations. This is good, for good men ought to live as God's witnesses against a wicked world. Good men are the best in wicked times and places; the best protestants are those that live in popish countries. In Jeremiah 24, the prophet makes mention of two baskets of figs, the one exceedingly good, and the other exceedingly bad, which represented the state of the church in that day. When there were great corruptions among them, the good are ordinarily very good, and the bad are very bad. Now it is our duty to be burning and shining lights to a crooked and perverse generation. When we see intemperance abound, we should be more strict; when we see uncleanness not only overrun the land, but grow bold and impudent, we should be more severe and chaste. When you see people turn to atheism and neglect the service of God, resolve to stand more firm, "as for me and my house, we will serve the Lord." Evil times obligate good Christians to be much better. (4.) God makes use of the sins of wicked men to exercise the patience, and thereby to increase the reward of good men. Who would have known of Joseph's chastity, had it not been for the lust of Potiphar's wife. Without wicked men there can be no persecution, and if there is no persecution, how can there be any rewards for patience? In a word, had there not been persecution, where would the glory of martyrdom have been? God orders that when wicked men seek most to destroy the church, he makes it much more glorious. A great saying of a martyr was, "come you wicked heathens, bring more racks, more fire, more torments, for hereby you add to my glory." (5.) Lastly, the overruling providence of God appears in making the sins of wicked men, which were intended to frustrate his purposes, the very means to bring them to pass. What was more contrary to God's purpose of advancing Joseph than to let him be sold for a slave and thrown into prison? So, in the narrative of Haman and Mordechai in the book of Esther, there was Haman's envy, pride, malice, and barbarous design of destroying all the Jews, and yet God made all these cross providences a means to preserve and advance his church. Therefore, beloved, God can do good to his church and children through them that intended no such matter. Jehu was a means to bring about great reformation in Israel, to purge them from idolatry; but did Jehu have any such intent? No! His intent was all about personal gain. Another example is Cyrus who, like other heathen princes, sought his own wealth and glory. Yet he is said to be the Lord's anointed, and to be raised up for the sake of Jacob his servant. How many times has God made the lusts of men and the ambitions of men to serve his own ends? The papists say it was the lust and ambition of Henry VIII that brought about the reformation. And, of course, we do not deny that God can make use of these to bring about good ends. We read in Acts 8 about a great persecution against the church, and what was the end God had in it? It was to scatter the disciples in all parts of Judea and Samaria, to take the gospel further abroad. If it had not been for this persecution, they may have continued too long in Jerusalem, (See Phil. 1:12). Seeing the effectiveness of Paul's ministry, the devil causes him to be put in prison. But what was God's purpose and end of it? "Those things which happened to me are fallen out to the greater advancement of the gospel, so that many of the brothers being confirmed by my bonds, have been so much bolder to preach the gospel without fear." The church of God, like the vine, flourishes when cut and pruned, and the blood of the martyrs watered the seed of the church. I could give you instances of this providence of God in many private persons, where the malice of their enemies has been a means to bring them to the highest advancements. I could tell you of a person who was falsely accused of a murder that once his name was cleared, the emperor took notice of it and advanced him to captain, and afterwards he came to be emperor himself. How many may say they would have missed significant life opportunities had they not suffered certain difficulties? And therefore, I have cleared up this most excellent point, and there is not a point of greater use for vindicating the honor of God's providence.

Section 4: Application

I will now draw some inferences from this text that may have an influence on either our instruction or the government of our lives when we suffer from the sins of wicked men. I will handle them by way of observation.

The first is that God almighty is just and holy and good, even in his governing the sins of wicked men, and the intent here is for the purpose of vindicating the holiness and justice and purity of almighty God in his concurrence with the sinful actions of men. It is one of the most difficult points in religion and one of the greatest depths of the providence of God to clear up. I will begin with the narrative of Joseph being sold into Egypt. Here are two concurring causes: his brothers sold him, and yet God sent him. As Acts 7:9 states, "the patriarchs moved with envy, sold Joseph into Egypt." I will here clear up God's justice in this matter. There was first a determination and decree of God to advance Joseph for the preservation of Jacob and his family. To bring this to pass, God makes use of his brothers and their envy and malice to sell him into Egypt. God does not infuse malice into them, nor stir them to sin, for that was in their hearts before. But neither does God hinder them. You heard before how when they first determined to murder Joseph, God would not allow it to go that way. But when they decided instead to sell him, he did allow them, because that supported his ends. Observe how God ordered that the merchants to whom his brothers sold him happened to come by that very day. Why this affliction is attributed to God and not to them is a hard question, "it was not you that sent me hither, but God," but the reason for this is that God permitted it. He offered them an occasion in his providence which he knew would take effect; and therefore, it was said, "God did it." I will, as briefly as I can, open and answer this statement: in all the sins of the world, let God be true and every man a liar. We must abhor and detest all that in the least attributes any sin to be God's, for God neither infuses wickedness nor tempts or stirs up people to sin. At the same time, his providence permits, orders, and governs it for his own wise and holy ends. I will here answer some objections briefly.

(1) You may wonder how it can be consistent with the holiness of God to permit sin when he can prevent it. I answer that it can be no stain to God's holiness, for God leaves the creature to the liberty of his own will. And those whom God has made free and reasonable creatures should not be constrained. But God does leave wicked men and devils to their own wills, especially since he can bring so much good out of evil. You may also wonder why God uses circumstances in his providence? It is reasonable that God should test the obedience of his creature to him, but that could not be demonstrated if he did not leave them to their own wills.

(2.) Most of the occasions and circumstances that men abuse in order to sin are inherently good and naturally would drive them to goodness; for what is it that they use to harden themselves with, and abuse to sin, but the very blessings and mercies of God.

God orders that sin serves his own glory and the good of his people, which is not contrary to his holiness or justice. So, what is more reasonable than that God should bring glory to himself from wicked men and devils also, that he should force glory out of them, above and contrary to their intents. It is an instance of the great wisdom, power, and goodness of God, that there is no evil that he cannot regulate and order for good ends. But then you may object. For doesn't the Scripture say, God stirs up wicked men, and blinds them, and hardens them, and sends them strong delusions, that they may believe a lie and be damned? How can this vindicate the purity and holiness of God? I answer, that in some places it includes a mere permission of God that includes a withdrawing of his grace and leaving men to the temptations of wicked men and devils. Secondly, God never withdraws his grace from wicked men until they, by their former sins, have deserved it. So, Pharaoh first hardened his own heart, and then God in a judicial way hardened his heart also. Beloved, what is more reasonable for those who resist God's drawing, and give themselves up willfully to be seduced, that God should turn them over to the seduction of the devil and wicked men and allow them to be punished by their own sin.

The next and greatest objection, and most popular in all ages of the world, is when God allows wicked men to prosper in evil ways and afflicts good men in good ways. This was the great objection of the heathens, especially the Epicureans, and it has been a great stumbling block to godly men. I remember four holy men in Scripture that were shaken and almost overthrown by the thought of it: Job (Job 21:6), David (Psalm 73), Jeremiah (Jer. 12:1), and Habakkuk (Hab. 1:13). Certainly, to heathens, and such as deny future rewards and punishments, I do not know a greater objection. But to this I answer, (1.) It is certain that this life is not intended by God to be the place of punishments and rewards, but only as a preparation for another life. (2.) No person was ever so righteous that their own conscience does not convince them that they deserve punishment. (3.) When God advances wicked men and gives them success, it is not for their sake, or out of love to them, but because he raises them up in his providence to be his instruments to punish other wicked men. He does not give them success as a reward for their behavior. Now, beloved, this is the most reasonable thing in the world, in all kingdoms the vilest of men are used as executioners, and indeed there is none fit for this work but the wicked. Does a shepherd stir up his sheep to worry one another? Godly men are not fit or qualified to kill or plunder other men unjustly; therefore, I say, God does not make instruments of wicked men for their own goodness, but because they are the only ones fit to be God's executioners. I remember a story about when Phocas murdered his master, the emperor, and made himself emperor, that a holy man complained why God should set so wicked a man over the nation. The answer was that they did not deserve a better emperor. It was for the same reason that God sends Turks to oppress Christians. Further, the man who now sees Pharaoh so stout and Herod so proud, should stay a while longer and to see one drowned in the sea and the other eaten up by lice. Again, though God allows good men to be afflicted by the wicked, it is for their good; it is to prepare them for God and glory, to rub off their rust and rubbish, and fit them for God. And lastly, I say as Augustine does, on the day of reckoning there will be no similarity between the prosperity of the wicked here and their sufferings hereafter and likewise, between the sufferings of good men here and their eternal happiness. The world is round, notwithstanding all the hills and mountains in it, because all these hills and mountains, compared to the circumference of the earth, are nothing. So, the sufferings of the good, and the prosperity of the wicked, may seem great to us here, and yet when compared to eternity, they are nothing. Suppose a person is condemned to death for high treason, and his friend comes and makes him merry and drunk, so that he forgets his condition. Do you envy this poor man this happiness, when perhaps in two or three hours he will be hanged? Likewise, if you could see a wretch in hell after 40 years of prosperity on earth, he would tell you he had paid dear for his happiness. Therefore, the prosperity of the wicked on earth is no more a stain to the holiness of God than the beams of the sun are diminished by reflecting off a stinking dunghill. It was an excellent saying of Dionysius, things that are seen in the hands of second causes, when they once come to God's hand, he turns and orders them to excellent purposes. Those things that are unjust regarding men, are righteous as instruments in the hand of God's providence. Suppose your child or servant proves to be wicked and disobedient. This is not a good or worthy thing, but they can be used as instruments to punish your sins, and in that way, they are just. I will conclude this first inference by stirring us to contemplate and admire the goodness, wisdom, and justice of God's providence, in governing the actions of wicked men. This is the masterpiece of God's providence, as Isaiah 27:29 states, "This also cometh from the Lord of hosts, who is wonderful in counsel." Here we see in the highest sense, Sampson's riddle verified, that God can bring meat out of the eater, and honey out of the carcass. And though we now complain about atheism, debauchery, and wickedness, at the last day God will make manifest how all these things have worked together for the glory of God and the good of them that serve him.

The second inference is this, that the concurrence of God in the sins of wicked men does not excuse their sin nor diminish their punishment. I am here, beloved, upon another deep point of the providence of God, that his providence, his decrees, and his ordering and governing of sinful men do not in the least excuse them from guilt or punishment, though God brings good out of their evil. Paul proposes and answers the question in Romans 3:7, "If the truth of God has more abounded through my lie unto his glory, why then am I reckoned a sinner, and not rather as we be slanderously reported? And some affirm, that we say, 'let us do evil, that good may come,' whose damnation is just." To restate, why should God count them sinners, or punish them as sinners, that have been instruments to serve his providence? This objection is made not only among heathens, but also Christians. You may say, "This sin was not my fault. If God had not put me in that situation, I would never have done it." I remember a story of a woman, a harlot, that had three bastard sons which afterwards came to be very great and eminent people. When she was brought to the point of confessing her sin of harlotry, she said she could not confess herself to be sinful in this matter, because her sons proved to be all such brave men. But I will refute this opinion by these five considerations.

First, the providence of God is not to be the rule for our actions. The guideline for our actions is his commandments, not what he does in his providence. As Augustine said, "We may will what God wills in his providence, and yet sin." A parent lies sick, his good son is troubled and uses all means for his recovery. God has decreed his death, so the parent dies and the son is troubled. Although in all this the son does no wrong, the outcome does not agree with God's decrees. On the other hand, a wicked son may wish his father's death and God decrees it so that he dies. Although this son's will is agreeable to God's secret and providential will, it is at the same time sinful. The rule for our actions is not what God wills, but what God has commanded us to do in his word. If God's providence would excuse sin, no wicked men or devils could be guilty of sin.

Secondly, I answer, wicked men do not aim for the glory of God in their sins, nor at the good God intends to bring about by them. Their aims are different from God's aim, as Joseph said to his brothers, "You thought evil against me, but God meant it for good." In Isaiah 10 the prophet warns that God would send a heathen prince against the hypocritical nation of the Jews to punish them, but of course, the heathen prince does not intend to do God's will; he is only interested in enlarging his dominions.

Thirdly, the good that follows from wicked actions is not a natural effect of sin, but comes only from the overruling power of God, and so is merely accidental to the sin. For example, no creature can bring good out of sin. When a man sins, he is said to break God's laws and in so doing reproach and dishonor God himself. Now if God, contrary to the nature of sin, brings good from it, sin is still sin, just as poison is still poison even when a wise physician uses it to concoct an antidote from it to expel poison.

Fourthly, it follows also that God is righteous to punish wicked men, even when they are instruments to serve his providence by their sins. God may use them, and yet they deserve punishment because God punishes them for their evil intentions and not according to the effect of their sins. Herod and Pilate and Judas all went to hell when God was done with them; also, Absalom, when God used him to punish David, took him away.

Lastly, does not the intention of God's glory excuse the sin? I answer, no; the sin is not any less sinful in that instance, as Romans 3:8 states. For God does not need our sins to bring his glory to pass, and God will not have us break his commands out of a pretense to bring to pass his glory. It is not lawful, not even for the greatest glory to God or good of mankind, to commit the least sin. To break God's laws for God's glory is not lawful on any pretense. For this reason, they that deceive and cause injury to others under the pretense of doing good with what they get and bringing glory to God, is nothing but a delusion and deceit. "But thou hypocrite, what need has God of thy robberies to do him service?" For this reason, the Jesuits have determined that in defense of the catholic cause a man may tell a lie because it is to a good end to carry on their cause. I will show you something of their doctrine about equivocation, from their own writers. (1.) It is determined that lies, when they injure none and do good to others, are, at worst, excusable sins. So, if they tell a lie for the preservation of themselves, but especially for the honor of God and the good of their society, it is but a minor, pardonable sin. This is what most of the papists believe. (2.) They tell us about the doctrine of equivocation, that some things, as they are spoken, are directly sins; but if we keep any other true sense in our minds, it is reconcilable to truth. Again they tell us that some things a man is bound to deny, and that under oath, if a priest from confession knows anything of adultery or murder in another, and he is examined in the matter, he may lawfully withhold the truth, or deny it, because he knows this under the seal of confession. They made great use of this doctrine in the gunpowder treason. They hold that when they are called before an unlawful judge, they may lie and forswear. They especially believe that no civil judge can judge a priest. They also believe that if they are accused before a judge, and the crime is not clearly proven, and if they have any way to evade the witnesses, they may lie and contradict themselves with a mental reservation, until the case becomes clear. They even believe that at their executions they may deny their crimes too, because when they have confessed to a priest, and received absolution, they are in a state of salvation, absolved from their sins. Therefore, fix this in your hearts, that for the greatest good in the world it is never lawful to commit the least sin.

Section 5

My third inference is this, if all the sins of men are ordered and governed by God, the only true way to secure ourselves from hurt by wicked men is to make our peace with God. It also follows that if all the sins of wicked men are ordered, limited, and overruled by God, the most secure method in all troubles is to make our peace with God. For if God be ours, all the malice of the devils in hell and wicked men on earth will do us no harm.

The first lesson we are to learn under every rod is to believe and trust God's hand in it. It is a thing, beloved, that we all acknowledge in theory though it is certainly one of the hardest things to practice. In Micah 6, the prophet tells us that it is the greatest part of wisdom to bear the rod and him who has appointed it, for the greatest cause of our stubbornness under God's heavy judgments is that men generally look no higher than the second causes. We attribute our troubles to our own negligence and the malice of men, but do not look to God. Isaiah 36:11 states, "When you lift up your hand they will not see it." Also, in Jeremiah 5:12, when the prophet told them God had sent the Assyrian to punish them, they denied it, and said, "it is not the Lord." Beloved, we tend to refrain from acknowledging God's hand in any affliction we suffer because it would be a secret acknowledgment of our own guilt. Thus, we are defeated in a war and we reckon it happened because of negligence or cowardice; or if a fire breaks out, we say it is due to the malice of men; we never look to God in all this. This is the great cause of our lack of repentance, for how can we repent of our sins if we believe we are only injured by men and not punished by God? We ought to believe there is no evil in a city but what the Lord has done. Whether evils come immediately from God's hand or from the malice, wickedness, and injustice of men, God has a hand in them all. Thus Job, when the Chaldeans and Sabeans had robbed him, he ascribes it to the Lord and not to their injustice. In Isaiah 10:5, when a plundering army was to be sent, it is said that God sent them. When Absalom rebelled and sought the ruin of his father, Scripture said that God would stir up evil to him out of his own house. In 1 Kings 11, when Solomon pursued strange women, God stirred up enemies against him. God sometimes raises up base and sordid men to be plagues and scourges to the most powerful people because of their sins. So beloved, if we are proud and confident in our own strength, our sins may expose us to be a prey to the basest nation in the world. Again, sometimes God limits the career of wicked men, as he does the proud waves of the sea, saying, "You can go this far, and no further." When God is done with his instruments, he will destroy them. It follows then that the greatest folly is when men seek to remove their afflictions so long as they continue in their sins against God, for what folly is it to look to the instrument, and not to the hand that moves it? It is as if a poor prisoner should court the executioner and not the judge. All these are our follies: first, we can with no reason expect God to remove his judgments while we continue in our sins. If God does cease judgments for a time, we must not take it as a pardon for our sins or a removal of our judgment, but only a temporary reprieve. If God withdraws one rod or judgment that we may fear, he will find new ones to chastise the wicked. As the angel cried, "one woe is past, and another woe cometh." So long as we provoke God, he will have new instruments to do his work. It follows therefore that the only safe way is to make our peace with God, for if he rules and governs all, then without him all the devils and wicked men in the world can do us no harm. If the Lord of hosts is for us, all the devils and the wicked cannot act without his permission. When a man's ways please the Lord, he makes his enemies to be at peace with him. When therefore we fear how we might suffer at the hands of wicked men, or when we are under their rule, then we are to look up and see God's hand in all and to make our peace with him. I am not saying that we are to neglect all prudent and careful means to prevent mischief from wicked men. For example, suppose they through injury take away our estates, or assault our lives, we are bound to use all care, and to seek the help of legal means to preserve ourselves. Further, magistrates are bound to use all possible legal means to oppose those wicked men that would hurt us. God has never promised to help the idle, slothful, and lazy, but those who are diligent and who use all probable means in complying with God's providence. When God uncovers the plans of wicked men and puts into a nation's hands the means to prevent them and yet they will not do so, it is a fearful sign of destruction. Beloved, I have often thought what we should do in such cases, and the first thing we ought to do is look to God above all second causes and say, when trouble comes, is not the hand of God in all this too? There is indeed much treachery, malice, and cruelty in man, but is it not all ordered by a wise and holy God? The second thing we should do is inquire as to why the Lord is angry with us.

We should search what sin has gone before this judgment. When God cuts us short of our estates, we should remember how unthankful we have been for them and how ill we have used them. Thirdly, before we begin to deal with our enemies, we ought first to begin with our own sins, to subdue them, and implore God's help against them. A better indication of England's happiness would be to see us reform our sins than to see all our enemies under our feet (Psalm 81:13-14).

If God orders and limits the sins of wicked men, then our duty is hearty and fervent prayer to almighty God, for if he sends them, he has the power to take them away. Thus, penitent Ephraim cries, "come, let us return to the Lord, for he has wounded us, and he will heal us." In the same way Jacob, before he contended with his brother Esau, first wrestles and prevails with God in prayer. And Moses, when Israel was fighting with Amalek, his hands were lifted up to God in prayer. The good emperor Theodosius, when he had lain all night prostrate on the ground in prayer, having thereby overcome God, got an easy victory over his enemies. And, dearly beloved, I wish we had done so, or would do so, for I am sure this is one of the best ways to prevail with God under the circumstances we are in. You are all sensible regarding the danger we are now in, and as to the instruments, there has been as much wickedness used as was ever known in any nation, to contrive the death of a king and the subversion of our religion. For them, it is without cause at all, yet in regard to God the cause is most righteous; and if he should give us up into their hands, we must say that God is righteous in all his ways, and holy in all his works. We have long abused peace with luxury and other sins, so God may justly take it away from us. But above all, for living so negligently and being so lukewarm under that religion that God has given us, our wickedness will justify the worst judgments that can befall us. And yet, beloved, God is merciful, and has put some stop to the designs of our enemies. O! that we may now return to the Lord by true and unfeigned repentance. Our sins give strength to the papists and Jesuits. If we would only live up to the religion we profess, all the Jesuits in Rome and devils in hell can never do us any harm. A political reformation that punishes offenders or makes more severe laws is good enough, but the only way for God to rescue us is for us to be good and walk answerable to the gospel we profess. I have long thought that if God almighty wanted to make a full discovery of this plot, it would be a deadly blow to Jesuitism, and to popery itself. But we cannot expect it without a reformation of ourselves.

Again, if God orders all the sins of wicked men, then it is a foundation of true patience and comfort in all our sufferings to consider they all come from a holy, wise, and righteous God. Dearly beloved, I will give you one remedy against all discontents, fears, and troubles, and that is, to see God's hand in every affliction, and I will show you how to improve them. It was a true argument the saints used to content themselves with, so old Eli when he heard the sad news of judgment denounced against his family, said "it is the Lord, let him do what seems good to him," (1 Sam. 3:18). Also, David, when he was under great distresses, said "I opened not my mouth, for it was thy doing," (Psalm 39:9). He had a similar response when he was reproached by Shimei, whom the Lord sent to curse David. And holy Hezekiah, when he was told of the ruin of his house and kingdom, he responded, "good is the word of the Lord." And finally, our Savior, under his bitter agony, said, "the cup which my heavenly Father has given me, will I not drink it?" Chrysostom tells us that all the malice and rage of men, when it comes into God's hand, loses its sting. Plutarch wrote against those who deny the providence of God, and uses this argument, that by so doing they removed all comfort from God's people who were under affliction. If I believed the affairs of this world were ordered by wicked men, and God was only a bare spectator, I assure you I could not live with comfort one moment. But when I know that in all the confusions and troubles which they cause here below, they cannot do one thing more than what God has ordered and appointed, I lay myself down and rest in God's bosom: (1.) Because they are ordered by God, our sovereign Lord, and they can only do with us what he allows and wills. (2.) Though we do not deserve it from them, yet we have sins that do require punishment. (3.) Notwithstanding all these confusions, God can limit and overrule all as he pleases. (4.) And lastly, when I also consider that God can make all these things end in the good of his church, and make wicked men do his work and his service against their own wills, where is there any room for discontent? Whatever troubles come, what makes them bitter is when we consider the wickedness of the instruments. We are apt to say, O! that false servant, that treacherous child, if God had done this or that, it would not have troubled us. Why beloved, look at the text, it is not them, but God that did it, for holy and wise ends. To have a child or friend cut off by some unexpected accident is a great affliction; yet we must consider that nothing happens apart from the wisdom of almighty God. (Compare Deuteronomy 19:5 with Exodus 21:13.) God does not allow a sparrow to fall to the ground without his providence, and much less will he do so by men. All things that seem to be chance to us are eternally determined by God. I have heard many tender-spirited persons say, "Oh, I am afraid I have not done all I should in this or that matter." Like Martha said, "Lord, if you had been here, our brother would not have died." But when God signifies his will by the event, then we are to rest satisfied; for God knows how to order our ignorance and follies to his own holy and wise ends. Again, when we think about the injuries of wicked men, the best comfort is to quiet ourselves, as with David, "the Lord has sent this Shimei to curse David." When we see a deluge of wickedness overflow a nation, it is one of the greatest causes of sorrow to a good man, as it was to David, "rivers of water run down mine eyes, because men keep not thy law." It is a just cause of sorrow that you are all called to at this time, yet, beloved, we ought not to be too much grieved. God will not allow his holy name to be always profaned. God can make this overspreading of wickedness turn to the good of the nation. Proverbs 19:31 says, "The counsel of the Lord will stand." They cannot go one step further than God allows, and he can and will overrule them. Again, this will be of great comfort to us in all the riddles of God's providence, when we see holy men oppressed, and wicked men, for a time, prospering. In all these intricate providences, God almighty will bring to pass his own wise and holy ends. Adore the Lord when you cannot comprehend him. The wicked have one work to do, and God has another. Do not judge conditions by their present appearances, for if you had seen Joseph afflicted, and in the dungeon, how could you have ever thought that would have been the way to a throne? Therefore, do not judge God's works before you see the effects of them. God has a work and purpose, and it will be brought to pass. Let men oppose and cross it as much as they can, for it is one of the greatest aspects of wisdom to resign our souls to God in the darkest of providences, when we can see neither sun, moon, nor stars. "Lord, I resign myself to you, though I cannot comprehend your design at present." Lastly, because God works together with wicked men and turns all their actions contrary to their own intentions, we ought to do all we can to work together with God. I will show you how we may draw good from the sins of wicked men. When the sins of wicked men bring me to see my own sins, to watch and walk more closely with God, and to more diligently seek after heaven and heavenly things, then the malice of my enemies is a means to increase my grace. This is how I can draw good out of evil. So as we see wickedness abound, let us draw good out of it. We should see ourselves as witnesses for God and, as a result, live well in the midst of a wicked nation. When we see a deluge of drunkenness and the spirit of whoredom among us, we should strive to be so much more chaste and careful against all company that may tempt us. When we see a spirit of formality and negligence in the service of God, this should make us more fervent and to love holiness all the more. And when you see people behave profanely, as in omitting the Lord's Supper for years on end, this should make us more diligent to practice it. The best way to overthrow popery is to live well, like good protestants. By this means we may turn our present dangers to a good result if we thus repent, thus live, and thus pray to our God.

FINIS.

A Sermon on James 2

A godly, zealous, and profitable sermon on the second chapter of James.

"What does it profit, my brethren, though a man say he has faith, and have not works? Can faith save him? If a brother or sister be naked, and destitute of daily food, And one of you say unto them, Depart in peace, be you warmed and filled; notwithstanding you give them not those things which are needful to the body; what does it profit? Even so faith, if it has not works is dead, being alone. Yea, a man may say, Thou hast faith, and I have works: show me your faith without your works, and I will show you my faith by my works. Thou believest that there is one God; you doest well: the devils also believe, and tremble. But will you know, O vain man, that faith without works is dead? Was not Abraham our father justified by works, when he had offered Isaac his son upon the altar? Seest you how faith wrought with his works, and by works was faith made perfect? And the Scripture was fulfilled which says, Abraham believed God, and it was imputed unto him for righteousness: and he was called the Friend of God. Ye see then how that by works a man is justified, and not by faith only. Likewise, also was not Rahab the harlot justified by works, when she had received the messengers, and had sent them out another way? For as the body without the spirit is dead, so faith without works is dead also," (James 2:14-26).

I have chosen this portion of Scripture to discuss because there is great benefit in its true and right understanding, and the doctrine contained in it is essential for all Christians to know. First, because it directly and fully overthrows all carnal professions of the Gospel, showing that a common, dead faith cannot save a man. Second, because it is the principal pillar the papists lean on and the chief Scripture they pervert and abuse to prove justification by works and to overthrow the free justification we have in our Lord Jesus Christ through faith. They grab phrases the apostle uses like, "Abraham our father was justified through works." Also, "Rahab the harlot was justified through works." Likewise, "you see that of works a man is justified, and not of faith only."

It appears that the two apostles of Christ, Paul, and James, contradict one another, for Paul said Abraham was justified by faith alone, and not by works, and James said he was justified by works. Paul said, and proves by various and invincible reasons, that a man is justified by faith alone without the works of the law. James said, "You see that a man is justified by works, and not by faith only."

This seeming contradiction is in appearance only, for they both wrote by inspiration of the Holy Spirit who always agrees with himself. The reason we are confused by the two is that we are so dim-sighted that we can't see how these two servants of God jump to agree with one another without any contradiction at all.

For this reason, before looking closely into the words of the text as they are laid out for us, it is important to answer this apparent discord. Men may ask why these Scriptures appear to be so contrary one to the other. I answer that although there is no contradiction in the doctrine they teach, it is because of the diversity of the scholars they instructed, causing them to use a diverse method of teaching.

Paul dealt with those who sought justification partly by faith in Christ and partly by their own deeds, or the deeds of the Law, using this order.

First, he showed that we are lost and condemned in ourselves, and then justified and saved through the merits of Christ. Then after we are sanctified in him, we must demonstrate the fruits of our faith by a pure and holy life.

James wrote to another sort of men who confessed the free justification through faith in Christ. And yet they did not consider how all those that are justified are sanctified, how all those that are in Christ Jesus are new creatures, that they are born anew, no longer walking after the flesh but after the Spirit. He taught that the true lively and justifying faith brings forth the fruits of righteousness in a holy manner of living.

Now because this cannot be separated from the right and lively faith, James proves, in a backward fashion, that where the fruits of faith are lacking, there faith is also lacking. His point, then, is to show that all ungodly and carnal professors of Christ have nothing but a dead faith, which can in no way help or save them.

A second reason they seem so much to differ is because the different authors focus on a different aspect of the same subject. Paul labors to prove that the true faith joins us to Christ and thereby saves us. Whereas James says that a dead faith is a mere shadow of the true faith and therefore cannot profit a man.

A third way that they differ is in not using this word "justified" in the same sense, which I will show later.

Now I come to the text itself: "What does it profit, my brethren, though a man says he has faith, when he has no works, can the faith save him?" This is his proposition, and the matter he will dispute in the whole text following, that it does not benefit a man to say he has faith, nor does it profit him to boast and to make profession of such when he has no good works to back it up. The reason it does not profit is that this kind of faith cannot save him. Mark this well, for here is the first place where, because of the blindness and folly of the papists, they do not see nor understand that it is not the purpose of the apostle here to dispute whether true faith saves and justifies or not, but to show that those who have no good works only demonstrate that they do not have true faith in them. Therefore, whatever they profess, they cannot be saved.

For what benefit is it if a man has faith but no works? In this situation, James is saying that a faith without works is only a semblance and shadow of faith, and not true faith indeed. Further, he supports his proposition with sound reasoning and proof. The first proof is taken from this example he gives: "if a brother or a sister is naked and destitute of daily food, and one of you says to them, "Depart in peace, warm yourselves, and fill your bellies," and yet you do not share with them those things which they are in need of, how have you benefitted them?" This is the sum of the matter. If a poor man or woman who lacks clothes and sustenance comes to you and all you give them is well wishes and gentle words like, "God help you, God nourish you and send you relief," but you give them nothing, can this help the poor man or the poor woman? Shall they not still, in spite of all your loving words, chill with cold and starve with hunger, if every man does no more than you and gives them no other gifts? Why do you not see then, that mere words to the poor is no liberality at all for it does them no good, so in like manner a faith which is nothing but words and an outward profession of speech is dead.

Why do you not understand that a thing which is weak and dead can in no way have power to give life and to save? Observe well this comparison, that if that liberality which is only in words is cold and dead, and does not profit the poor, then it follows that that faith which is only in speech is dead, and therefore, cannot save or profit him which has it.

If words alone could profit or cause a living faith, why should not mere words also profit the poor man or woman who is destitute? If words alone can make a man have faith, why should not words alone give a man what he needs? If a man's faith has power to do the greatest things, like join us to Christ, or transform a soul from death to life, or put the devil to flight, or overcome the world, should it not make sense that *words alone* would be powerful enough to perform the lesser things, like bring forth good works?

Brethren, know that if a faith can do the former, it must necessarily do the latter. And if it is not sufficient to do the latter then surely it is dead and can do nothing to save. This is a most plain and forcible reason to prove that the faith of a carnal professor of the Gospel is but a dead show of faith, and therefore he is not justified nor saved. Neither can he be justified or saved by such a faith, seeing as it has no life in itself to bring forth fruits, so it cannot give life to him, for how can it bring that which it does not have?

To set this out more plainly, the apostle adds, "but some might say, you have faith, and I have works. Show me your faith without your works, and I will show you my faith by my works." Here he demonstrates how a simple man who is a true Christian may be able to deal with the greatest and most skillful doctor that is, to prove that he has no faith if he does not have good works, because faith is a holy thing, wrought by God's spirit, and a lively and mighty thing. Therefore, it cannot be without holy and good actions. For as a man is known to be dead when he does not breathe, cannot stir, see, hear, and such like. And to the contrary, when he does any of these, he is known to be alive. So it is with faith, if a faith is said to be alive and yet does not bear good works, then it is dead. And on the contrary, the actions and stirrings of a true and living faith show it to be alive.

This is strong proof against all those who boast of a vain and dead faith. It also provides proof for those who are of God and who are of the devil. If a man is found to wallow in wickedness, and you say, "you do not possess true faith because you are worldly, a drunkard, an adulterer, and such like." If such a one asks, "Who made you able to judge? You cannot tell how I believe! How will you take it upon yourself to see what is in my heart? I have as good a belief as yourself." Make a note how you should answer such fellows. For faith indeed is a secret thing in the heart. But because it cannot be true without good works, as James tells us, just like fire cannot be without heat, the Lord allows us to say, "show me your faith by your works." So that when your tongue is foul and your deeds are wicked, it is most certain that the heart is unclean and there is no right faith. For true faith cleanses the heart, as Peter says in Acts 15.

If you only go by men's words and outward boastings of their belief, you would be led to think that almost every man believes strongly in Christ. But come to this touchstone and trial which is given to us here, and that is, "show your faith by your works," and a different viewpoint emerges. We then say, "When the son of man comes, shall he find faith upon the earth?" This is true, because God himself has set it down: that the faith which is without good works is dead. Do you think that if the Son of Man should come now, that he would find any great store of faith? For how great the sinful deeds of most men are, which, according to James, only demonstrate that they have no faith. How few are the good works, even in the small remnant of the godly?

But we must go further in this matter and dig a little deeper. As men are willing to deceive themselves, so they will find a hole to creep out of and say, "It is true, God's word says that the proof of faith is good works. And I thank God, though I have many vices in me, that I am not altogether without good works. I am not so graceless that I do not sometimes remember God in prayer. I give to the poor as I am able. I am ready to befriend my neighbor. Do these things not sufficiently show that I have faith?"

Dearly beloved, take heed so that you are not deceived. The apostle is not saying that a sampling of good works among great heaps of sinful works will hold up no more than a few grains of corn in a great heap of chaff. For a true faith will be shown both in forsaking and renouncing all evil ways, and in following all goodness.

Without question, those that seem to be good works before men are not so before God. Can good come out of the same heart in which ungodliness reigns? The tree is either good (Christ says) and the fruit good, or it is evil, and the fruit is evil. A good tree cannot bring forth evil fruit (Matt. 12:13, Luke 6:43). Neither can an evil tree bring forth good fruit. Can the same tree bring forth both good fruit and evil fruit? Does a fountain at the same place (James says) send forth both sweet and bitter water? (James 3:11, 1 John 3:7).

Do not be deceived, John says, for he that works righteousness is righteous, and he that commits sin is of the devil. Some man will say, does not the godliest man that lives commit sin, and does not both good and bad together come from him? The godly are burdened with the corruptions of the flesh, it is true. But they do not continue to commit sin, that is to say, they are not given over, as ungodly men are, to the obedience of sin. They are spotted with imperfections, but they do not take pleasure in them as the wicked do. They are not perfect in good works, yet their whole intent is to do good works. They obey their God on both sides in forsaking all that is evil and doing all that he commands them.

Contrariwise, the wicked *gives himself over* to that which is filthy. And if he does anything which is good, it is done for show and not in sincerity. It does not come from a good motive, but of self-love, vain glory, or such like; he does nothing for the Lord's sake, but for his own. If you love him, you shall find him ready to do you good. But if you cease being good to him, his goodness toward you also dies. Praise him, and he will praise you in return; discommend him, and he will do nothing for you, even if you deserve to be praised.

Do not forget what I tell you here, good brethren, because God has given us so plain a test by which we may determine if one is faithful or an infidel. If we find ourselves full of good works, and our heart bears witness that we do them because of our love towards God: well are we, this declares our faith. But if our evil deeds abound, and our heart is unclean, it is time to look at our heart, for we are in a most miserable state.

I pray to God, that we might often think upon this, and be careful to show our faith to the world by our good and pure life. Do not be afraid to apply this to ourselves, and to use it do deal with the ungodly. For in this depraved age, where iniquity has almost gotten the upper hand, it is most necessary that we use this instrument which God has put in our hands: "If you say you believe, then show your faith by your works."

Now follows another reason in the text: "You believe there is one God: you do well: the devils also believe and tremble." Weigh this argument well, and you shall plainly see that it does nothing at all to help a man to say he has faith, when he has no good deeds: if this kind of faith could save him, then the devils would also be saved, because they have the same belief.

But because it is most certain that the devils shall not be saved, therefore it is also as manifest, that those men who have no other belief than that which the devils have cannot be saved. Let us see then how far the faith of devils go.

You believe, he says, that there is one God, or that God is one, and so you think this a great matter, not to believe as the vain Gentiles, which believe in many gods. And indeed, so far you do well. But mark what a great matter you have attained, that devils believe the same, and yet have no benefit or reconciliation with God, for they tremble when they remember the terrible judgement seat and the everlasting fire which is prepared for them. This faith of the devils is not to be restrained to some one point but stretches unto the whole doctrine of faith. They steadfastly believe and know that Jesus Christ died for the sins of the world. They know the doctrine of God when they seek to deface and overthrow it by contrary errors.

When a man is of sound judgment in the Scriptures for matters of faith and is able to confirm every point and to overthrow the contrary errors, many will say he is a sound man. Further, he takes himself to be as great a believer as any other. Yet if he has no works, if his faith is not a likely regenerating faith, he may believe of himself what he will, but the Lord tells us that he is no more profited than the devils, for they are as sound in the knowledge of truth as he is. And if this common and general faith would serve, they should be saved as well as he.

But it may be here objected, that there is a great difference between the faith of devils, and the faith of those men which believe and yet have no fruits of godliness in them. The devils believe all matters of faith to be true, but they do not nor cannot believe. They have no hope of mercy. But men, although they are very sinful, are in hope that they shall be saved. Here is a great difference therefore, that the faith of such men goes far beyond the faith of devils.

May the Lord give us eyes to see and hearts to understand, for I will show what the difference is, that the faith of devils is *more perfect*. For what is the reason that devils have no hope, and the wicked men think they have hope? Is it because they have less faith? No, it is because they are wiser, and because they give credit to that which God has threatened against them. They believe that he will pour out his wrath upon them because he has said it.

But wicked men are more foolish, and where God has pronounced eternal fire against them for their sin, they do not believe him, and so indeed their faith comes short of the faith of devils. They should believe the Lord when he tells them that all those which do not turn from their ungodliness, when he calls them to repentance, shall be cast into hell. But they blind themselves and seem to believe quite contrary to that which God affirms. I say this not to shut the door to repentance, but to move men to seek for it, while God offers himself, for they shall not be able forever, and only when they will. It is God which must *beget us* to himself, and give us the new birth, and sanctify us by his spirit to bring forth the true fruits of faith, and not to have a dead belief which changes us no more than the faith which the devils have changes them.

For there are many this day who being stuffed as full of wickedness as they can hold, and their words and deeds plainly show that they are no more changed then devils, will still brag of their faith and its strength as if there should be but ten in the whole country saved, they expect to be among them. And yet they never understood the doctrine which the Lord teaches here. God give us understanding that we are not seduced, but that we may seek at the hands of Christ to give us a faith which may differ from that which the devils have.

Here also shall appear the ignorance of the papists. They say that James speaks of the same faith that Paul does, and that he plainly affirms it does not alone justify. But see here as he said before, what does it profit a man to say he has faith and has no works? Can that faith which is but in words, or the dead faith save him? So now he tells us more plainly, what faith he is talking about, and it is that faith which cannot help a man, the same faith which the devil has. But is this not that same faith which Paul says justifies, worked by the Holy Spirit? Shall we be so blasphemous as to say the devils are partakers of him? You may well perceive therefore that James speaks nothing against that which Paul has proved, how Christ alone is our righteousness, whom we take hold of only by faith. For he shows that the dead picture of faith does not save. Remember well then what faith is here spoken of, and the controversy is soon decided.

The apostle now proceeds to his last reason, which because it is wonderfully strong, he uses it as a preface to it, lest we should pass lightly over it without due consideration. "But will you understand," (says he) "O you vain man, that the faith which is without works is dead?" See how vigorously he thunders here against the carnal professor, calling him a, "vain man." Likewise, can those former reasons satisfy you? Are they not strong enough to persuade you, or plain enough to teach you? I will share with you a reason that neither you nor all the world shall be able to refute. It is so strong and so manifest, that it will stop the mouths of all those who seek to deny it and force them to confess that the faith that is without works is dead.

See how marvelously the Holy Spirit labors to drive us from trusting this broken staff, and to force us to seek after the true and right belief, if we have any care to save our souls. And without a doubt daily experience teaches us how needful a thing this is. For the greatest number of professors suppose and will say that they believe well enough, that they feel no want at all. Indeed, this dead faith of theirs seems to them to be very strong. They believe it cannot be shaken, neither is it tried or tempted, for to what purpose should the devil labor to overthrow it? But those who have any faith indeed, feel the need to use all means to strengthen it.

But let us come further to the matter, for now he proves by examples that the true faith is known by good works. The first example is of Abraham. You know that Abraham was a holy man, and an upright man indeed. He was highly favored with God. The Abrahamic covenant was established with him, that in his seed all nations of the earth should be blessed. You will then confess that he had the right faith; there is no doubt at all in that. You must also agree that as there is but one God, one mediator, so there is but one faith. It follows, therefore, that as many as have such a faith, or the same faith which was in Abraham, shall be saved, and none else. For although every one of the children of Abraham do not attain to the same measure and strength of faith that their father did (Eph. 4:5, 1 Tim. 2:5), yet they are like him and have the same belief.

Then I urge you to observe well the second part, which demonstrates how the faith of Abraham was fruitful, declaring and showing forth itself by good works (Gen. 21). For he offered his son Isaac upon the altar. It then follows that all his children and all the sons of God declare and show forth their faith by their good deeds. And whoever does not, they are degenerates and bastards. None are his children, none are partakers of any blessing with him, for their faith is dead, and therefore they are not alive in Christ.

Do you see, dearly beloved, the marvelous force of this reason, and that it is as clear as the sun? There is no hole left for a man to hide himself in, nor to creep out of. The doctrine is clear that if a man will be saved, he must declare and show forth to the world by his good works a holy life, how he walks in the steps of his faithful father Abraham.

But why does he choose this one work of Abraham before all the rest? For his life was defined by holy works – he was merciful to the poor, he entertained and lodged strangers, he was peaceable with all men, just and true in all his dealings. But no doubt this one work excelled, and so far surpassed all the rest that it may be mentioned instead of them all. It declared a wonderful faith and love towards God, as we may easily see, considering all the whole circumstances of the story.

God called him out of his native country, and from his father's house, into a strange land. He had promised him a son by his wife Sara, of whom the blessed seed should come. He performed this promise in his old age, even when Sara was by nature past childbearing (Gen. 21:12). He had no other child by her, and the promise was made only in him, "In Isaac shall your seed be blessed."

Each man shall now be driven to confess, that this was a great test, when God told him to take his only son Isaac, and go three days' journey to the place which he would show him, and to offer him upon the altar as a slain sacrifice. How great a grief is it for a loving father to lose a son whom he loves dearly, especially when he has no more sons. Then how much grief might this be, not only to see his son slain, but also to slay him with his own hands, and most of all that child in whom the covenant of eternal life was made, because Christ should come of him. And if he is dead, then all hope of salvation would die with him.

And yet all this was not enough to cause Abraham to hold back from anything but full obedience, for the faith of Abraham carried such a great love and fear towards God that he never hesitated nor begrudged God's command, but following God's instructions went forward to slay his son. Having bound him upon the wood, as he raised his hand with the knife in the air to kill him, the Angel of the Lord from heaven stopped him. Before the Lord it was as if it had been done because Abraham fully intended to do it.

We see plainly by this what true faith is. If any man should object and say, this example is not appropriate because every man cannot be like Abraham, nor have such a faith as he had for he was a rare man and none should be compared with him, James answers that if you think this example is too high, and that you are not to be measured by it, I will show you another as low.

What would you say to Rahab the harlot? Was she justified by works? Did her faith not declare itself by good works? Can you take any issue against this example? Will you not be ashamed that your faith should not be like hers? As the faith of Abraham spoke itself to the world, so did hers. And in doing so, she showed herself to be a true daughter of Abraham, although she was not of his posterity according to the flesh, but came from one of those cursed nations which God commanded the children of Israel to root out and destroy. And yet I say, she was his daughter, according to what Paul sets forth in the Epistle to the Romans, that he should be the father not only of them which are of the circumcision, but also of those that walk in the steps of the faith of our father Abraham like all his children, both of the Jews and Gentiles, which will be blessed with their faithful father Abraham.

Then we have here the example of the father of all the faithful, with the example of one of his daughters, which had been a poor harlot. What excuse remains? Shall we not blush and be ashamed to say that we believe well, and take ourselves to be the children of Abraham and the children of God, when we are no more like him than (as the common saying is) an apple is like an oyster? Christ our Savior uses this reason against the Pharisees in the Gospel of John, "If you were Abraham's children," (he says), "you would do the works of Abraham. But now you go about to kill me, a man that has told you the truth which I have heard of God, something Abraham was not able to do." And a little later he tells them, "You are of your father the devil, and the lusts of your father you will do." What could you have plainer than this? Even the very seed and posterity of Abraham, which took themselves to be the children of Abraham and the children of God, Jesus tells them plainly that they are the children of the devil, and why? Because their works were not like the works of Abraham; their belief was not like his either, but it was dead.

Shall we not then as boldly tell ungodly men to their face, no matter how you brag of your faith, it is dead? However you boast and take yourselves to be the children of God, unless you return from your ungodly ways and show forth the fruits of a true and lively faith, you are the children of the devil. Do not trust in your vain hope and dead faith, for it will only deceive you.

Dearly beloved, let us not be so mad, when God tells us this with his own mouth, to believe the contrary, and to persuade ourselves that we shall do well enough, although we continue in our sins. This is a most pestilent craft of Satan, and comes from the root of infidelity, as you may see in our great grandmother Eve. God told her and Adam, that if they should eat of the tree, they should die the death. The devil told her, "you shall not die," and she believed him instead of God. She thought even as the devil told her, that she should do well enough, or else she would never have eaten the fruit. We have sucked this poison from her, because when God tells us, "if your faith does not bring forth good works, it is dead, it cannot help you. And if you continue in these wicked deeds, you are the children of the devil. You must speedily repent, for you cannot simply repent whenever you choose."

"No, no," says the devil on the other side, "that is not true. Your faith is good enough. You shall do well, for God has mercy in store. You may repent afterward." Now most people believe the devil, and give no credit at all to God, and never seek to test themselves, whether they are in good standing or not.

When the apostle says here that Abraham was justified by works, and that Rahab was justified by works, *etc.*, we must note that this word "justified" is used different ways in the Scriptures, which is one reason (as I noted before) why Paul and James seem to contradict one another. Paul is proving that we are justified by faith, in contradiction to this word "condemned," for being found guilty by reason of our sins to justly receive the sentence of condemnation, we are in Christ (into whose mystical body we are incorporated thorough faith), acquitted and discharged from condemnation. This is what Paul is referring to as justification, and this justification cannot be by the works of the law, because there is no perfection in the deeds of any, but even the purest are unclean and spotted.

Therefore, as Paul says, they are all under the curse, for it is written, "Cursed is every one which continues not in all things which are written in the book of the law to do them." The reason for this is because of the most holy and pure nature of God, unto whom no unclean thing can be coupled, and no impure thing can abide his presence or have fellowship with him.

The word "justify" is also taken in this sense, when a man declares and shows forth before men that he is a righteous person also before God. That is the meaning of the word in this place, that how by faith we are justified before God, so by the fruits of our faith we are justified, that is, declared to be just before men.

For proof that the Scripture uses the word "justified" in this sense, look what David says, "That you may be justified in your saying, and pure when you judge." In this passage it signifies that God declares himself to be just. In Luke 16:15, Christ says to the Pharisees, "You are they which justify yourselves before men, but God knows your hearts." Here it is clear that there is a justifying before men, which the Pharisees in hypocrisy sought. But Christ tells them that they were never the better, because they were not of an upright heart before God.

The word is also taken in another sense, which I have here omitted. But if any man will now demand how it can be proved that James uses it in this latter sense rather than in the former, I will answer that when the apostle says, "Some will say, show me your faith by your works," is it not apparent, that he speaks of that which is before men or declared unto men, and not of that which is before God?

In the same manner, when he says, Abraham was justified by works when he offered his son Isaac upon the altar, does not the Scripture show that before God Abraham was justified long before by faith? If it is contested as to how he was justified before men before that time, or that he showed by his deeds that he feared and loved God, then should it not also be acceptable for a more full and perfect justification, that he is accepted before God as he is before men?

I answer, that when a man is justified before God, to speak properly there is no increase of faith from that point, for he is fully and wholly discharged and acquitted once for all, or else it is not justification. But because we have received the grace of justification in part and not in full measure, our justifying before men is more and more declared by degrees, as good works more and more abound in us, and so Abraham was by this one work more justified before men than by all the rest of his deeds, which is why it is more than enough to show his faith than of all the rest. We see here then that because this example must necessarily be taken as an increase of justification in our father Abraham, that it should be understood to be that justification which is before men.

Now you see the meaning of this text and the angle and scope which the apostle has laid open for you. But there is yet more to observe, which is a more particular application and handling of this doctrine which we should not overlook.

You will confess these things which I have handled already to be true, so we also agree that the Holy Ghost has given a perfect touchstone. Then I am to exhort you in the name of God, as you nurture the salvation of your souls, to give attentive heed a little further, and not let this thing slip away from you.

Do you agree that the faith which is without works is dead? And that it is no better than the faith of devils? And yet will you still suppose that idolaters, swearers, railers, adulterers, covetous men, usurers, and such like are in good standing and can hope for mercy when they choose?

Do you confess that there is but one true faith, which was the faith of Abraham and Rahab? Do you also acknowledge that the same faith in them showed itself by good deeds? Then how can you accept it to be a sufficient proof of a good and sound testimony of true belief when any man can say, "I harm no man, I live uprightly, and pay every man his due, I have always been reputed and taken for an honest man, so what more would you require of me? I live as my neighbors do. I trust God will hold me excused." And yet this man has no regard for obedience to the word of God, to consider wherein his glory consists. He does not care for other men, to profit either their souls or their bodies, but contents himself with this, if he does them no good, it is the same as doing them no harm.

I will show you, dearly beloved, how these sorts of people are deluded by two foul errors, which this text strongly overthrows. The first is this, that they look to men, and consider their duty to them, whereas they should chiefly look to that which they owe to God, and then to that which belongs to their brethren. The second is that they suppose themselves bound no further but to abstain from hurting, without regard to the duties of love where one man is to profit and further another.

As concerning the first of these, both the example of Abraham, and also of Rahab, manifestly convince them, because the fruits of their faith or the works by which they were justified did not so much respect man as God. In Abraham there appeared only a love towards God, for whose sake he was contented to forget the affection of a father and to show that although he loved Isaac dearly, yet he loved God more. So that if we feel our love to the Lord our God to be so small that it cannot move us to kill and mortify the lusts of sin and vain pleasures of the flesh, how shall we persuade ourselves that we are like Abraham, who denied the love of himself so far that he never begrudged God's command, but willingly would have killed his son.

Rahab, after confessing what she believed concerning the God of Israel, for God's sake, for the true religion, and for the church and people of God, took the messengers of God and hid them to the hazard of her life and all that she had, affirming to the king when he sent to seek them that they were departed. Does this kind of faith not rise far above the faith of those who for the religion of God are so far off from risking their lives and goods that they dare not be seen when even such a little danger arises? In what way are those like Rahab, who turn with every wind? They are sure to row with the tide, and never to strive against the stream. Do such now justify themselves like Rahab? Do they have a similar faith to hers?

No, dearly beloved, they are still infidels, and love themselves and the world more than they love God and his truth. This then is most evident, that true belief makes all those that have it ready and willing to lose their lives and their goods for the Gospel. This must not seem to be a strange doctrine, when our Savior tells us in different places that he that does not forsake all, and take up his cross and follow him, cannot be his disciple.

We must therefore be so zealous in the profession of true religion that it causes us to forget our own state. We must have such a burning love for God's truth that nothing may be able to quench the same. We must not stagger and vary, because we endure trouble. Let us conclude this point, in which it is proved that those who do not keep their religion pure, loving it above all things and in so doing give God his due honor, err greatly.

Remember that the true description of a godly man and the test of justifying faith is but one. Therefore, works are similar in all those who are partakers of that one true faith, though not in the same measure.

But mark how far the Holy Spirit shows the difference between a righteous man and the wicked. He shows it to be the chief work of respecting God himself and his truth. The wicked bypass that and count it no matter that a man is an idolater, or superstitious, or a swearer who does not reverence the name of God. Yet he is a friendly man to his friend, and such like. But how great an enemy he is to the word of God! These are brute beasts without understanding, atheists which will say plainly they can see no difference between the papists and the professors of the Gospel, both because they are not able to judge the doctrine, and also that they only consider good works before men.

Now let us come to the second thing they err in, and which this text sharply refutes. They suppose (as I told you) that men are to have no further regard but this, not to harm others. They may pass by all those duties where they would do good to their brethren, not considering how the law of God does not only bind us to abstain from hurting our neighbor, but also does most straightly bind us to do all good deeds to them. This is why the man is just as guilty before God who not only commits the sin that the law forbids but also leaves undone what the law instructs. True faith moves us to obey God wholly.

James requires that a man show his faith, not only by leaving that which is evil, but also by the performance of that which is good. For in this way he says, "Show me your faith by your deeds," and that "faith which is without works is dead." Observe here by comparison how far off those are from grace who are full of unclean vices, doing nothing but continually sinning. And yet those men who carry some great show of uprightness by refraining from various vices are still without the testimony of true belief because their holy deeds do not appear.

As the holy Scriptures testify, the heart is purified by faith in those who are born again by the new, spiritual birth. They are new creatures and have a new heart and a right spirit, created and renewed in them. It must needs be, therefore, that they are prepared for every good work. They have not only put off the old man with his corrupt lusts but have also put on the new man which is created in righteousness and true holiness. And as they have walked in darkness, so now they walk in the light.

There is one step further in this matter. I trust that as you will confess this, that if those do not believe well which have no good works to show, although they be in some things upright, and much more those foul and filthy sinners who dishonor God and his truth, so you will also be brought to see that those miserable men are further off still who rant against this holy doctrine. These men may say to the wicked and ungodly, "you are on your way to hell, you shall die the death if you do not return from these evils." They may thunder and rail against men, uttering damnation. But let them see if they can quench the light which the Holy Ghost has given in this text.

Let us return to the former matter again. We must not only abstain from evil, but also do good. Many are deceived in their doing good, restraining it to the baser and lesser part. They consider the physical needs of their brethren and assume they have no further responsibility to them but to relieve and ease the miseries of the flesh.

Let our soul never be so blind, so sick, in so great danger of eternal destruction, that we have no pity for the soul of men by looking no further than this life. These have no true love nor pity in them, for if they did, they would love the souls of men which are so precious. They would pity the woeful misery that so many are in.

For how absurd a thing is this, that one should be careful to ease the calamity which lasts only a day, and not respect that which is eternal? I must therefore here again admonish you, that he that will have proof of their faith by good works must exercise the same to both the physical and spiritual needs of others. And because it demonstrates the greatest love of all other, they are to prove themselves most earnest.

There is no more excellent proof of faith and of the true fear and love of God, than when a man is grieved and mourns to see men running headlong in their sins toward destruction, and when he does, in love and pity admonish them and seek by instruction to draw them out of the snares of the devil.

On the contrary side, he can never say he has one drop of grace who delights and sports himself in the lewd and wanton behavior of other men. Judge, dear brethren, these foolish men who laugh at the sinful and profane speeches of vain men. Do they show the fruits of faith? Those abominable men who delight to make men drunk so they may laugh at them. Are they of God or of the devil?

We must diligently exercise the contrary, laboring to draw one another to God and to convert their souls which go astray. This is the chief good work that we can do to men. To feed the hungry, to clothe the naked, to visit the sick and those who are in bonds. To open the bowels of mercy and compassion to all that are in misery are very excellent and glorious fruits of faith and have great promises of reward in the holy Scriptures.

Yet are they not comparable to when the soul is sick and imprisoned by the chains of Satan, to visit and relieve it? When it is pining away for want of heavenly food, to minister to it? When it is full of grievous sores and deadly wounds, to give healing medicines and salves, to mourn with the bowels of pity and compassion for it?

For here is where hearts sob and groan with sorrow. When they see men left without instruction and when they behold the desolations and ruins of the Church, it pains their heart. It causes bitter tears to flow out of their eyes when they behold any famine and death of the food of life, and when they see them run from sea to sea, and from the one end of the land to the other seeking for it, and when they see the young man and the beautiful virgin perish for thirst.

He that doubts or denies this never knew what the use and benefit of the word is, nor what that love in the spirit is, which the Lord expects of us. I might go on to show the cruelty of those parents who allow their children to be without the knowledge of God and to perish in their sins. For one of the chief fruits of their faith stands in this which the apostle commands in Ephesians 6:4, "Fathers provoke not your children to wrath, but bring them up in the nurture and instruction of the Lord."

    For those who have the riches and wealth of the world, the Holy Spirit says in 1 John 3:17, "He that has this world's goods, and sees his brother in need, and shuts up his bowels of compassion from him, how can the love of God dwell in him?" If it is true that the rich men of the world do not love God when they will not part with their riches to relieve the misery of their brethren, no doubt it is a stronger argument against them when so many souls perish for want of good and pure instruction, which by their wealth they might accomplish if they did not care more about their riches than the salvation of men. If God's word pronounces those blessed who use their goods to feed the poor, then how much more blessed a thing is it when they are employed to the ministering of spiritual food which never perishes?

    But let us come to those which have the charge of souls. What is the principal good work which they are to show their faith by and to declare their love towards Christ and his Church? In John 21:15 Jesus asks Peter, "Simon son of Jonas, do you love me?" Then feed my sheep, feed my lambs, feed my sheep.

When the hireling is overseeing the flock of the sheep and lambs of Christ and does not feed them, or at the least feeds them in a way that they are never the better, where is the faith that they boast of? Can it be anything other than dead faith and the faith of devils? Whoever therefore will have the testimony of his faith in this calling must execute the office as the Scripture binds him.

Is it possible that he can give credit to the word of God, and be of a right belief, and not regard this? The rest of his good deeds by which some will say he shows his faith are not good deeds. For if he did them out of love towards God and his brethren, would his love to both not show itself? Can he love God, and hate God at the same time? Can he love men, and hate men at the same time? Or can he love God, and not commit to do his will? Can he love men, and not care for the salvation of their souls? O my brethren, who cannot say to such a man, "Show me your faith by your works?" Who will be so blind as to think such men have the true faith?

I will now bring this to a close, exhorting every man while God gives him time and ability to give himself to the exercise of good works and the service of God. And dear brethren, what better place to begin, as our time is short, than with this passage. For is it not a marvelous blessing to have this witness of our faith? Is it not a miserable curse to be without the true peace of conscience and to live in doubt? Does God not also promise that, although we can deserve nothing, when we have done all that we can and we are still unprofitable servants, that all our good works shall be rewarded (Matt. 10:42, Luke 12:33), even to a cup of cold water given for his sake? Shall not the promise of reward move us?

How dear and precious the name of our God ought to be to us! How much it should delight us to hear it magnified, and how much we should grieve to see it stained and dishonored! His name is honored when those who call upon him are fruitful in good works. In John 15:8, Christ says, "Herein is my Father glorified, that you go and bring forth much fruit." Also, he says, "Let your light so shine before men, that they may see your good works, and glorify your father which is in heaven," (Matt. 5:16). For the same reasons, God's name is dishonored by the evil conversation and behavior of those which profess his word, as Paul spoke about in Romans 2:24, "The name of God is evil spoken of through you, among the heathen."

Should not the Gospel be dear to us? Otherwise, when the wicked see the evil deeds of those who profess Christianity they can say, "These are your Christians, here is their holy doctrine, these are those who seek after sermons. You may see what they are, and what their teaching is. They have as few good works as other men, they are all just words."

These things should move us to let the world see our faith and love towards God by our good works! For there is no greater love which can be shown towards men, than when they shall be moved by our good deeds to glorify God. In the day the Holy Ghost visits them, our good deeds should cause them to confess that it is a holy religion which we profess, and so they give ear and join themselves to the same.

It is a happy man whose holy life is a means to draw others from their evil ways, and to bring them to be scholars in the same school that he is. Contrariwise, what a woeful and miserable wretch is that man who slanders and dishonors the holy word by his sinful life that drives others from it and pushes them headlong to destruction. Shall not the blood of these in some sort be laid to your charge when you drive them from the Lord and his truth headlong to destruction?

I might mention many particulars, but then I should be over tedious. The Lord plant these things in our hearts and give us grace to continue in all goodness to our life's end, to his glory and our eternal comfort. Amen.

FINIS.

A Sermon on James 3

"My brethren, be not many masters, knowing that we shall receive the greater condemnation. For in many things we offend all. If any man offends not in word, the same is a perfect man, and able also to bridle the whole body. Behold, we put bits in the horses' mouths, that they may obey us; and we turn about their whole body. Behold also the ships, which though they be so great, and are driven of fierce winds, yet are they turned about with a very small helm, whithersoever the governor wishes. Even so the tongue is a little member and boasts great things. Behold, how great a matter a little fire kindles! And the tongue is a fire, a world of iniquity; so is the tongue among our members, that it defiles the whole body, and sets on fire the course of nature; and it is set on fire of hell. For every kind of beasts, and of birds, and of serpents, and of things in the sea, is tamed, and has been tamed of mankind. But the tongue can no man tame; it is an unruly evil, full of deadly poison. Therewith bless we God, even the Father; and therewith curse we men, which are made after the similitude of God. Out of the same mouth proceeds blessing and cursing. My brethren, these things ought not so to be. Doth a fountain send forth at the same place sweet water and bitter? Can the fig tree, my brethren, bear olive berries? either a vine, figs? so can no fountain both yield salt water and fresh," (James 3:1-12).

There are two things contained in this portion of holy Scripture. The one is a precept against rigorous judging of our brethren: the other is for the ordering and guiding of the tongue in general. Men offend generally and commonly in them both, and the offences that are committed are not light, but very grievous in the sight of God.

Regarding the former, committing this sin will cause one to receive the greater condemnation. The severity of the offences committed in the other is manifest by the words of the apostle in which he talks about the poison of the tongue. And in the first chapter of this Epistle, verse 26. he says, "If any man among you seems to be religious and does not bridle his tongue, but deceives his own heart, that man's religion is vain." It is evident here that these matters are of great importance, and so I urge you to hearken attentively to the voice of our God and make effort to obey the same. Otherwise we deceive ourselves, as he says in the first chapter, regarding those who hear the word only and do not obey. Doubtless considering how common the vices of the tongue are, and how the Lord here warns against them, it is astonishing to think that there is any true religion to be found among men, seeing how many rigorously judge and do not bridle their tongue.

But let us come to the words of the text. "Be not many masters, my brethren, knowing we shall receive the greater condemnation: for in many things we sin all." There are three branches in this: the first is the precept,

"Be not many masters, my brethren." The second is a threatening of terrible vengeance, if we do not avoid that vice, which is found in these words, "Knowing that we shall receive the greater condemnation." The third gives reason why men should not be severe in judging their brethren, because if they are, their judgment will be heavier before God as he says here, "For in many things we sin all."

Regarding the first branch, which is the precept, "Be not many masters," James speaks somewhat vaguely in this, because *Master*, or *masters*, represents an office in the Scriptures. Christ is called master, and rightly, for he is the great master. "You call me," he said to his apostles in John 13:13, "*Ho didaskalos*, master and Lord, and ye say right, I am so." And Paul said that Christ had some apostles, some prophets, some evangelists, some pastors and *didaskalous*, that is doctors, teachers, or as it is translated here in James, *masters*.

Some take the word here to mean the public office of teachers, and especially because he said, "be not many masters." For in saying, "be not many," it seems that he allows the mastership which he speaks of here in a few. Otherwise, if being a "master" is a vice in itself, why does he not say, "My brethren, let no man be a master?" Thus, it seems that he warns against that great vice of men being so ready to throw themselves into the ministry, when they should not do so, seeing as they are unfit. So, the apostle here urges us that many should not enter the public office of teachers, as God gives gifts only to a few, which allows them to be able to discharge it well.

But indeed, here he does not deal with that public mastership, but with a vice where each man takes it upon himself to be a severe censurer, a judge, and a condemner of others. For in doing this, men take upon themselves to be masters. The apostle might more plainly have said, "Let no man be a master," seeing no man may be a severe and rigorous condemner of others.

Here he is applying his speech according to the sin which he reproves, for almost all take it upon themselves to be masters, that is, to assume the judge and control of others. As in the diseases of the body, if a man has an infirmity, he can find many physicians, for almost all men and women will have some medicine or another to prescribe, even when they do not know the complexion or constitution of the body or what has caused the disease to grow. Though sometimes they are right, often they miss and do more harm. If one should say then that there should not be so many physicians, it should be clear this statement applies only to those who are unskillful in ministering to the sick.

And so here, when he says, "Do not be many masters," he both notes the vice to be common and reproves all those rigorous condemners of their brethren. It is as if he should say, "Let not this fault remain, that there are so many masters." This does not apply to those who are gifted to be masters, for it is only the fault which the Savior forbids and not the office itself (Matt. 7:1-2).

Men are naturally sharp sighted and curious about other men's faults. They will pronounce them very hardily and rigorously. Moreover, they not only judge small faults to be major offences in others, but also twist that which may be well done or well construed to cause it to appear divisive. It is almost a religion with some to construe faults even in the best men, causing them to glory and feel as if they are great masters, exceeding all others.

Such men sharply find fault, and in so doing please themselves as men in a more perfect estate. Of these it is written in Proverbs 30:12, "There is a generation which is clean in their own eyes, which are not washed from their filthiness." These are become such great masters in their own eyes that they despise being taught by anyone. They are masters, which means in their eyes, that they are no longer disciples of any. So, if a man does not please them, no matter how excellent that man is, he is worth nothing to them.

Against this uncharitable and unbrotherly severity, this warning is added, "Knowing that we shall receive the greater damnation." This shows how much God is displeased with that kind of man, because he threatens such heavy judgment against him. In this warning God is purposely trying to terrify men from such a foul sin, one in which they take pride in as if it were a virtue. For they oftentimes flaunt it, as if it were a zeal of godliness against sin in them.

On the contrary, this teaches how much it pleases God if we judge the frailties of our brethren with charity, pity, and compassion, and with that spirit of meekness which the apostle requires, (Gal. 6:1). The reason both of these appear in the words following the third branch, "For in many things we sin all," is because that even based on their own judgment against men which they so rigorously speak, the judgment of God is just against them as well, as they have the same faults or even many times greater, as our Savior confirms when he asks "How can you see the mote in your brother's eye and miss the beam that is in your own eye?" (Matt. 7:5). This is the state of those who nitpick the faults of others, they observe small things in their brethren and condemn them with rigor, while covering and mitigating with excuses such vile offenses in themselves.

Shall not the judgment of God be just and severe against them? About this matter Paul reasons, "You are therefore inexcusable O man, whoever you are that judges another, for in that you judge another, you condemn yourself, for you do the same things which you condemn others for. We know that the judgment of God is according to truth against those who do such things. Do you think, O man, who judges those who do such things, and you do them also, that you shall escape the judgment of God?" (Rom. 2:1-3).

We might reason that if a sinful and corrupt man condemns others as evil men not worthy to be spared for such and such sin they commit, then how shall I escape the judgment of the most just and righteous God, seeing I am also guilty? We may hear some that profess the gospel swear some oath which is a common fault to be condemned. For the holy Scripture is plain, "Do not swear." Then those who refrain from swearing will be so rigorous, and uncharitable, and so severe in judging that swearer that he is void of all religion and fear of God. And in the meantime, they do not see the vainglory, self-love, bitter wrath, and anger in themselves, that if it is stirred is as hot as fire, and brings with it many other foul sins.

If motes (as our Savior called the smaller frailties and faults in men) are judged by us so severely, then how can such foul and loathsome sins in the judgers escape the sentence of God? This proves that he who is a rigorous judge against his brother cannot escape the severity of God's judgment, because he is also guilty in those things for which he condemns another. May this truth mitigate our severity. May this move us into a moderation in our sentence which we are so ready to give others when we see them slip. For it should be in our mind when we look at ourselves that we sin in many things and are full of imperfections.

I would have the Lord to show mercy and pity towards me. I would not have men rigorously judge me but deal with me charitably and compassionately. Shall

I not then, when I see my brethren in the same condition, be favorable towards them? Would I find mercy at the hands of God? Would I have men charitable towards me? And yet without mercy, charity, or compassion I judge them rigorously, while being in the same state as they are.

Judge in yourselves brethren, is it not the same thing? For in many things we all sin. So, if we would have mercy and compassion shown us, we should then lay aside rigor and show mercy and compassion towards our brethren who are weak and frail, and subject to many temptations. How perverse is it that I should think myself worthy to be pitied, and not others, and that I would have all men deal charitably towards me, and I return no charity to them? I may speak about others as I wish, but if any speak badly about me, I will not have it.

As we look at these great masters which James mentions here that nitpick daily at the faults of others, we see that when they have whipped other men with the scourge of the tongue, and pierced them as with a sword, that if any dares to say the least thing about them, as slight as the prick of a pin, watch how they react and call for charity. They do not consider what they do to their brothers when they make small faults out to be heinous offenses and perversely deprave what was well done by others. But woe be to that man who speaks a word against them, as that is a grave injury that should have been dealt with in charity.

What a high value such men place on themselves while basely esteeming others. Such men look at others as not to be regarded or pitied because of their sins, and yet they, having the same sins or greater, are still very precious. In this we see how far men are from where they ought to be. The Lord calls us from it, and it is our duty, if we will be wise, to seek to be cured of so grievous a disease. It is a precious and acceptable thing to God when we consider and judge of ourselves among others, in such a way as to see ourselves with them as poor sinners to be pitied, and so become pitiful also and full of mercy towards them. For this is what the Lord said by the prophet, "I will have mercy and not sacrifice," (Hosea 6:6).

We must be sure that it is charity and mercy that we show toward our brethren, and not some irreligious covering of sin or soothing men in their evil ways. For under pretense that we are not to judge, many will choose to reprove no one and leave every man to himself. This is contrary to the doctrine of the holy Scriptures, which urges us to admonish one another. It is contrary to the rule of charity as it is written, "Do not hate your brother, but plainly rebuke your neighbor and do not allow him to sin," (Lev. 19:17). And our Savior Christ when he says, "Judge not," is not saying that we should not admonish and reprove our brethren for their faults, if we do it rightly. He doesn't say, "Why are you meddling in the faults of others or why are you concerned about the mote in your brother's eye," but rather why are you judging their smaller offenses without judging your larger ones? He instructs us to first cast the beam out of our own eye so we can see clearly to cast the mote out of your brother's eye.

Here is the matter. If we are to be right reformers, we must begin with ourselves. For how can we be fit to teach others if we do not teach ourselves first? What good can come from that? Can a man be concerned that another should be saved and be godly, and not care for godliness and salvation in himself? Can he pity the souls of other men if he does not pity his own? Again, what manner of rebuking is it that rigorously points out another's fault while overlooking their own?

In this we can see a great difference between Christian and charitable admonishing and rebuking which the Scripture commands, and that rigorous judging which it forbids. For regarding the one, he that is truly reformed and knows the grace, the mercy, and the love of God, he is moved with mercy and compassion towards others and wishes their reformation to their good.

This allows him to look at the faults of his neighbor whom he loves and wishes well and when he does something amiss, he can speak to him friendly about it. This sort of reproving is much appreciated. We all thank God when he gives us the kind of friend who will remind us of our duty. For we can see other men's faults, and other men can observe our offences more clearly than we can see ourselves.

In worldly matters men are very willing to find fault and to be taught where they have gone wrong, so they can see that profit come to them or gain thereby. Shall we not be as willing to be informed of what may benefit our souls?

Regarding those masters which James speaks of, their doing is nothing like that. They are not reformed themselves. They notice faults, they judge others severely, they nitpick, they object. But not out of pity or compassion, not respecting the good of those whom they judge but to defame, discredit, and bring them into contempt. Do you not think it strange that these men, void of charity and full of great sins, should consider themselves of a more perfect state than others, and take upon themselves a mastership, with a right to judge so severely and to point out men's faults? Do not be surprised, beloved, that the Scripture thunders warnings against this kind of people, for their doing is abominable.

It is true that a wise man, when any of these "masters" spread reports of his faults, frailties, or imperfections, or when they reprimand him with the same to his face, does not consider what their intent was, but how true it is and if it is true, seek to amend it.

For this reason, if we are wise, we can profit from the hard speeches of uncharitable reprovers, for by them we can hear of imperfections which our friends are blind in, and it causes us to be more cautious in our doings, when such severe judges observe us narrowly.

The second part of this Scripture now follows, which deals with the ordering and guiding of the tongue. And this has two parts: the former part discusses how the ordering of the tongue carries such a force with it, although it is but a little member, and how all is well ordered when it is right. And to further explain, two examples are given that show how small things direct and order great things – the bit of a bridle and the rudder of a ship.

The second part declares the exceeding power that the tongue has when it is not well ordered to all mischief. Where it might seem strange that such infinite evil could proceed from such a small thing, he uses an example from a spark of fire, from which such a large area is set ablaze. Further he shows by comparison to the most wild and cruel things what a horrible unruly evil the tongue is.

"If any man sin not in word, he is a perfect man, and able to bridle the whole body." In this proposition, which is hypothetical, he shows that he who is able to rule his tongue so that he does not offend with it is perfect, and bridles and orders well the whole body. For where that little member goes right, all goes right.

But is there any man perfect? Who does not sin? If by "a perfect man" James means one who has no sin in him, then he is putting forth a case that is impossible. For without a doubt, if it was possible for a man to be perfect in his tongue, he would be perfect throughout.

The Scripture calls "perfect" those men who are come to a sound strength of godliness and ripe knowledge of God, as in 1 Cor. 2:6. "We speak wisdom," says Paul, "among those which are perfect." And Phil. 3:15, "As many as are perfect..." And Heb. 6:1, "Let us be carried on to perfection." If we take perfection to be so, then observe that the measure of a man's godliness is how well he controls his tongue. For the perfection or the lack of perfection in the whole man directly aligns with the lack of perfection or perfection of the tongue. Our Savior Christ shows the cause, saying "Out of the abundance of the heart the mouth speaks." A good man out of the good treasure of his heart brings forth good things: and an evil man out of the evil treasure brings forth evil things," (Matt. 12:34-35).

The tongue is the special instrument to utter everything which is in the heart. To the degree the heart is sound and good, this is the degree to which the tongue will be good. For let the heart proceed to sin, and the tongue will utter it. Let the heart be good, and the tongue will reveal the goodness of the heart. Whatever evil is on the tongue can be found in the heart. And when wicked thoughts are in the heart, the tongue cannot hide it, but will at one time or another reveal it.

Regarding particulars, if the heart is full of light, knowledge, and true wisdom, the tongue will utter it. If there is darkness, ignorance, and error, the speech will show it. If there is faith, the tongue will confess it. If the love of God, there will break forth praise and thanksgiving. If meekness, the words will be gentle. If pride and wrath, the tongue is fierce and bitter. If chastity, then pure speech, and from unclean lusts, a foul mouth. The tongue is as the heart in all things. A vain tongue reveals a vain heart.

Let no man stand and say, "words are but wind, it is no great matter what a man's words are, there is no harm done; it is just communication." This is an ignorant position, for the words are of such weight that our Savior said, "You must give account for every idle word on the day of judgment. By your words you shall be justified, and by your words you shall be condemned," (Matt. 12:36-37). Shall a man then say further, though my words are vain and foolish, yet I mean no harm, my heart is good? What kind of imagination is that? Does not the tongue reveal what lays hidden in the heart? Even as a man beholds his face in a glass, so may we behold the heart of a man in his tongue.

It is true that the hypocrite who has a wicked heart can speak good words, yet the wickedness will break through at every chance. But shall such a little member extend as far as the apostle here indicates? Shall the man who bridles it bridle all parts of the body?

This is no wonder, as he declared by his two examples. Horses that are strong, fierce, and full of courage can be turned about by a rider when they have a little bit in their mouth. A ship is a great thing, and often driven by fierce winds upon the seas, and yet the governor with the little rudder turns them about which way he will. As such little things turn about great and mighty things, so the tongue. Though it is but a little member, it boasts great things.

This seems to be a very hard application. For he speaks of the well ordering of the tongue and what power it has, and now he says it boasts great things. For boasting is not good, and a man may boast great things that he cannot do as great things. The bit in the horse's mouth turns him about, and so does the little rudder boast of turning about the great ship. Why then does he say the tongue boasts great things?

James uses it here not as boasting that is evil, but to say "look how the bit is a little thing and turns about the whole body of a fierce horse, causing him to obey the rider. And the rudder is small and still turns about a great ship. As these two little things do great matters, so the tongue being a very small member lifts itself up to the performance of very great things. It boasts that it performs them indeed.

But what are those great matters which it does so well? To speak briefly, it brings forth all the good treasures of the heart, as our Savior said. Look what gift of grace or heavenly thing the Holy Ghost works in the heart of man, and his tongue utters the same. The tongue is given as a special instrument to glorify and praise God. What a great duty it is to perform that way, and as it were to lead the whole body. The tongue is also able to do many good things towards men.

A wise heart brings forth wisdom and knowledge to inform and to instruct the ignorant by the tongue. It gives wholesome advice and good counsel to such as need. It persuades and comforts, exhorts, admonishes and rebukes as required. Yes, infinite are the benefits which the tongue rightly ordered brings men. "Let no corrupt communication proceed out of your mouth, but such as is good to the use of edifying, that it may minister grace to the hearers," (Eph. 4:29).

And he says, "Let your speech be always gracious and powdered with salt, that you may know how to answer every man," (Col. 4:6). Beloved when we consider these things, it teaches us how far off we are from perfection. For how often do we come short of guiding our tongue well to the performance of these great things, both in glorifying God and also in ministering grace by our talk at all times to men. If we do well and thoroughly discern them, this one thing would be obvious to us, that in many things we all sin, so that we might not be so rigorous in condemning or judging others. For if we fall so far short in the duties of the tongue, both in praising God and also in benefiting men, how can we number all our sins? We may well say that they are more in number than the hairs of our head. But why has the Lord given this much power and good to the right ordered tongue? It is not that we should come to see how imperfect we are, but that we should strive towards greater perfection. It is a most worthy thing to profess the holy faith and to sound forth the praise and glory of the most high God. Also, it is an excellent thing to speak such words that minister grace to the hearers. To this end, Solomon says, "The tongue of the just man is as refined silver, and the lips of the righteous do feed many," (Prov. 10:20-21).

Now that I've spoken to the first part, which is the ordering of the tongue aright, I will proceed to the other part, which is the unbelievable harm of the evil tongue. For in the same way that the power of the tongue to do good is great where it is well ordered, it has just as much power to do evil where it is not bridled. And in case this seems hard to believe, the apostle uses a comparison. "Behold how great a thing a little fire kindles." We all know that one little spark of fire is enough to burn a whole house, and so a whole city, a country, yes, the whole world, as much as will kindle and burn. This is a phenomenal thing which God has given to the fire, that from so little, such great flames will arise and spread in this way.

And James says that the tongue is fire. It is not our common fire, of course. Rather it is figuratively called fire for it will spread far, though it be little, and set everything in its path aflame even as fire. Yes, it extends itself in mischief so far that he calls it a world of wickedness. What a strange saying this is. Is the tongue so small a member, and yet contains in it such a depth and such a gulf of all wickedness? A world is a great thing, it is the universality of all creatures, and the holy apostle uses this image to express the wickedness of the tongue, as if he should say, "the generality of all evil and wickedness is the tongue." What evil, what mischief, what wickedness, what treacheries and lies do not come from the tongue? Mark how he says that the tongue is so placed or set among our members that it defiles the whole body. If a thing is full of evil, but far enough away that it cannot touch another thing, then the evil is not spread but simply defiles itself.

 But it is not so with the tongue, for it is so set that it defiles the whole body. Fire does nothing when the dry matter is absent. But if it lights on it, then it enflames all, and sets the whole thing on fire. Even so, he says that the tongue reaches and sets on fire the course of nature. The whole course of nature may very well be taken for the whole world, as if he should say, "The tongue even like a firebrand sets the whole world on fire." The truth is that in all places where there are hot flames of contention, there are broils and dissentions. Yes, all things boil and burn with the fire of the tongue.

 And in the next words he shows what kind of fire the tongue is and where it comes from. It is itself set on fire of hell. The tongue is not only fire, but it is a most pestilent and hellish and devilish fire. Hell enflames the tongue, but how can that be? Hell is for the devils of hell, they set the tongue on fire. They enflame it with hellish fire. As the Holy Ghost inspires and sanctifies the heart of a good or godly man, and fills it with all precious and heavenly treasures for which the tongue brings forth praise and glory of God to the benefit of men, so the devil fills the hearts of wicked men with such treasures as hell affords, and their tongues utter forth the same.

In that respect the holy apostle says that the tongue itself is set on fire of hell. O! that men would consider how their tongues are the special instruments of the devil to spread through the whole world the fire of hell. O! that they would weigh and consider who they serve and whose work they perform. That tongue which is the chief instrument in the body of man to magnify the praise and honor of the Lord and to benefit men, how is it turned and changed to be the firebrand to set the whole world on fire, even with the fire of hell?

What is this fire which it is enflamed with, and with which it enflames the whole course of nature? You know that Paul says the devil has fiery darts which faith quenches. Where there is no faith, he fixes those darts in the heart of man. And so, when the heart is filled with that hellish fire, the tongue presently receives it and casts it abroad like wild fire. He shoots the dart of pride and vainglory and ambition into the mind, the dart of selflove, of envy, of hatred, and of malice. Moreover, he fastens his darts of vanity and vain pleasures with the darts of all unclean lusts of fornication and adultery. These are from hell, these are fiery, and the fire of God's wrath is with them. The tongue scatters and disperses all this fire abroad. Words of contempt, of disdain and reproach, words full of fury and bitter rage, with lying, and slandering, and backbiting, words full of vanity and horrible oaths, words full of filthy raciness and all manner of ghastly things.

Shall I try to number the stars or measure the sands of the sea? If not, why should I try to enter into all particulars in this matter? There is nothing which the fiends of hell suggest to the wicked hearts of men that the tongue does not pour forth. Here we see that all the world is on fire, even with the fire of hell. There is cursing and raging; there is boasting, quarrelling, and reviling; there is false accusing, lying, and condemning. As the apostle said before there is in the speech a world of wickedness. All the parts of man are defiled by the same. It is a general contagion that overspreads the whole. And James further shows the unruliness of the tongue by a comparison. There is a wonderful fierce nature in various sorts of wild beasts, as in the lion, the leopard, the tiger, and the wolf, along with many others. And yet some of these, men have caught and tamed. There are also among the fowls, among the creeping things, and among the fish, wild and unruly creatures which men have tamed.

But James says the tongue, no man can tame. The cruel nature of the savage wild beasts, fowls, serpents, and fish, is not like the tongue that surpasses them all. No wisdom or power of man can tame that. Is this not a strange thing? Will men believe that this little member should have such a nature in it, that no man can rule it? Do not marvel at this. The cause is evident, explained earlier in this text. Is there any beast, any fowl, any serpent, or fish, whose nature is to be compared to the devil or to the fire of hell?

No doubt, every man will say there are horrible and savage natures among beasts, and serpents, and dragons, but the devils go beyond them all. There is no comparison for hell cannot be matched, that fire cannot be quenched. There is no taming of those things. Then mark how he said that the tongue is set on fire of hell. The nature of hell, the nature of the devil is put into the tongue. This is why it is harder to be tamed than all the nature of serpents and wild beasts. Then he says, "But the tongue can no man tame." The tongues of the prophets, the tongues of the apostles, the tongues of the martyrs and holy men have uttered the heavenly truth to the praise of God and to the singular good of men. How then is it said, "The tongue can no man tame?" Were the tongues of these not well tamed?

Yes, but it is still true that the tongue no man can tame. For their tongues were not tamed by themselves, nor by any wisdom, power, or virtue of man, but by grace, by the working and power of the heavenly spirit of God from above. None but the Lord God, whose power is above all, has ever tamed the nature of the tongue. There is nothing in man from Satan or from hell, no matter how pestilent and horrible, but the grace and power of God can subdue it. By saying that the tongue no man can tame, the apostle is leading men to let it alone. For to what end and purpose should a man try to do that which is above his power? I say it is not the purpose of the holy apostle to persuade, but by showing it to be impossible regarding man's strength, he moves men to seek God for the power of his grace. For therein is all the help. And seeing there is help in God, how can we be excused, if we do not flee to him?

This thing is most horrible. We should abhor the fact that we carry in our mouth the fire of hell and the nature of the devil. Rather, shall we not thirst for those heavenly and pure waters of the Holy Ghost, which extinguishes such hellish fire? O beloved, it is the mind and purpose of the apostle when he shows us these things, to stir us up to seek God more earnestly and not to trust to our own strength. For we carry a firebrand with the venom of a serpent in our mouth.

How loathsome should it be to the mind of every man to have his mouth full of the fire of hell with the ability to cast it abroad? It would seem strange if any beast should carry rank poison in his mouth that he could cast far and near. But the tongue of man spreads something that is a great deal worse than any poison. For men spit fire, even the very fire of hell. Should we not seek help for this?

Beloved, do not be deceived in thinking that the words of the apostle are stronger than the matter requires. I confess that the holy Scripture sometimes uses hyperbolic language, but not in these comparisons. It is true that the tongue is indeed, as he says, an unruly evil, full of deadly poison.

You know what is written in other places, "Their mouth is full of cursing and bitterness, the poison of asps is under their lips, their throat is an open sepulcher, they flatter with their tongues. Should we not loathe carrying such horrible deadly poison in our tongues? Let us think well of these things, and judge them, as the Lord pronounces, and not according to our own sense: for as everything loves that which is in their own nature, so men by nature love the poison which is under their tongue, and that fire with which it is enflamed by hell. Men glory in those horrible things which come from their tongue. Let us therefore, as I said, judge the things as the Lord pronounces, and not according to our own sense. The Lord says that the tongues of men are full of deadly poison. If we were thoroughly persuaded of this truth, would it not force us to seek the Lord to have such poison removed? Would we rather continue as venomous serpents? Could we think well of the fact that the devil should fire our tongues with the fire of hell? Or that he should use our tongues as his instruments to set all in a broil?

God be merciful to us, and help us, for our case otherwise is most wretched and miserable. And let us now see what reason the apostle gives to show that the tongue is full of deadly poison, for he gives an instance or a taste of the same deadly poison in one particular, sense which is this: "therewith bless we God even the father, and therewith curse we men which are made after the image of God. Out of one mouth proceeds blessing and cursing. My brethren these things ought not so to be."

If he should stand to show the poison in every instance, it would be too much. There is almost none so wicked but will have words of praising God in their mouth. Men's words are often so godly and smooth that they seem to be with devotion, even as if they carried a reverence and a great regard of the name of the most high God. But let any man displease them, and sooner or later they will curse him. This shows that their blessing and praising of God is but a vain show. For if they did indeed love and reverence the majesty of God, then they would also regard his image in man. For man is made after the image of God.

Can they bless God and curse his image? If we bless and praise the Lord in all his works, then we should chiefly in the workmanship of man, in whom he has set the print of his own image. And if we cannot in that work behold his glory and praise him, how shall we do it in other things? To be sure, the image of God was broken down in man through the fall of our first parents. And that for those who are renewed in Christ, and the image of God again established in them, in those we may behold the glory of God.

And yet the tongue curses the good as well as the bad, and spares none. And doubtless, it is a greater and a fouler thing to curse a right godly man than to curse a wicked man, because in the godly man, the image of God shines in beauty, and where his image appears greater, we are bound more to love and to reverence.

But it is also a sin to curse any man because he is still also made in the image of God. For even though the image of God concerning righteousness and holiness is broken down wholly in them, yet there remains some part of his image, there is understanding or reason, and such things in which a man greatly differs from a beast. And that is why James describes this as an absurd thing, that the same tongue blesses God and curses men which are made after the image of God.

This cursing is especially common where wrath is kindled and displeasure arises. The horrible curses and insults which come out of men's mouths would make a man that fears God tremble to hear. There is no sparing of any, but this deadly poison of the tongue is poured forth on all. The brother curses the brother, the father the children, and the children again their father, the husband the wife, and the wife her husband.

If a man defiles his mouth and the ears of those that hear it, he might utter enough usual curses and insults to fill a book. And let two men or two women fall out, mark the bitter poison of the words which will come from them. What insults will each one give the other? What words of disdain, contempt, and reproach? How base will each of them set forth the other to be? Whatever can be devised that is base, vile, and loathsome, one will decidedly use it to harm the other. There is no more regard of the image and glory of God in each of them, then there is of a dog. What a poison is this? What a vile wickedness proceeds from the tongue!

James shows that it is a monstrous thing to pervert the order and course of nature, when out of the same mouth proceeds both blessing and cursing. Does a fountain send forth at one place sweet water and bitter? Can the fig tree bring forth olives or an olive vine produce figs? Of course not, and neither can one fountain produce both salty water and sweet. If this is against the course of nature, then how can it be that some words which come from the mouth are as sweet water, and some of them are bitter. They should all be either sweet or all bitter.

Now it is most evident that the cursing of men, the contemptuous railings, reproaches, and insults are not sweet, but as most bitter water. It follows that the other part which seems to be very sweet water, that is, their blessing and praising of God, is also very bitter. For as the holy apostle shows, they cannot be both sweet and bitter. If one is bitter, both are bitter.

But how can their blessing of God be bitter? How can that be poison? Is not the blessing and praising of God, a most precious and a most excellent thing? Does James put that with the poison of the tongue? I answer that the blessing, the praising, and the honoring of God is of all other things the most excellent and precious when it is rightly done. But if it is done for show, or in mere words, it is a profaning and an abusing of the most holy and glorious name of God. Then is it hypocrisy, then is it sin, yes, even an abomination.

We read in the Gospel that Jesus would not allow the devils to confess him. And the devil in the maid that uttered this saying regarding Paul and his companions, "These be the servants of the most high God, which show unto us the way of salvation," displeased Paul (Acts 16). These leave no doubt that the praising or blessing of God with a wicked tongue is not acceptable unto him.

Make note of how James has reasoned to prove that God is not blessed nor honored by a tongue which curses men. First, if they did sincerely and from the heart bless God, how could they curse the image of God in men? Secondly, it is impossible in the course of nature, that sweet water and bitter come out of one fountain, and so it is that true praising or blessing of God, and cursing of men, cannot come from the same mouth.

Let us all, then, consider how we honor and worship God. For when men claim to be religious, and they call upon God, they ascribe glory and praise unto him. They never consider what manner of tongue they do it with. They curse, they rail, revile and reproach. They swear, they lie, they slander and defame. They flatter, they boast, they scoff, they pour forth words of all vanity. They speak all manner of unclean words, and out of their mouth comes forth communication as if it were a stinking filthy puddle or rotten dunghill.

And then with the same polluted tongue, and in that unclean vessel of their mouth, they offer up those sweet odors of the praise of God. This great instruction is ministered to us, which we ought carefully to hearken to and to print in our mind. If ever we have dealings with any man or woman who is poor and base in outward respects, and take it that they offer us wrong so that our wrath begins to be kindled, let us take heed that neither our heart so far despises them, nor our tongue utters such contemptuous words to them, such words of disdain and ignominy, such base and vile terms indicating that we forget the image of God in them.

O beloved, how grievous a sin is it that we attribute terms to the image of God that we would scarce give a dog? If any shall object and say that some are so wicked and abominable that no speech can be too base for them, I answer this: according to the doctrine of the holy apostle here, that however we abhor their wickedness, however we may express their bad estate (as the holy Scripture does), we should yet regard the image of God in them, even so far as it remains, do not curse or revile them lest in doing so you curse, revile, and utterly despise the image of God.

To conclude, let the fear of God bridle our tongues, that this deadly and devilish poison may be taken out of them, and that with them we may magnify and praise the Lord God, so that our praise may be acceptable unto him and that our speeches may be such as tend unto edification and minister grace to the hearers. Amen.

FINIS.

A Treatise of True Fortitude[12]

To the Right Honorable and his Very Good Lord, the Earl of Essex.

Among all the virtues, there is none more profitable and, in every respect, necessary for the safety and good of human society than fortitude. Her fruits are such that those kingdoms and commonwealths are blessed whose princes and nobles are valiant. For there truth, justice, and peace shall flourish, lacking no good thing.

The fame of this noble virtue is so great that many men seek her, their chief study and primary concern being how they may become valiant and brave-minded men. But the greater number of them, for lack of good direction, in the end attain a foul vice instead of a pure virtue which they embrace and make much of. It is a great pity that the mighty courage found in many men is not set right. They do not know how to climb high to the royal palace of this goodly virtue but imagine that they can find her without knowing her properties. I have therefore written here a few things (so far as my small skill may serve) to give some light in that direction.

---

[12] *A Treatise of True Fortitude*, by M. George Gifford, Preacher of the word of God, at Maldon in Essex. (London: Printed for John Hardie, and are to be sold at his shop in Paul's Churchyard, at the sign of the Tiger's head, 1594).

It is true that this virtue of fortitude is out of my reach to handle in the worthy manner it deserves. I wish, with all my heart, that some would take in hand to draw her picture in accurate symmetry and proportion, and with her lively colors in a way that even the great princes and nobles might take pleasure in. Since I come so far short of this, it may seem rash and worthy of much blame, that I presume to offer such a rude and slender discourse to the hands of your Honor. But I think I can remember sufficient reasons to excuse my boldness.

First of all, I am assured of this, that the virtue fortitude is so beautiful of herself, so well favored and so comely, that she does not need to be ashamed, not even in her most base attire, to show herself in the presence of great princes.

Secondly, it is the common hope and expectation of our whole land (at least those who demonstrate faithful hearts toward their prince and country and love the truth), that God has prepared Your Honor as a right worthy instrument, furnished with a heroic spirit for the defense of our most noble Queen and kingdom.

Thirdly, I know that such a poor treatise will be little regarded among many, and so if there is anything in it worth the knowledge, it may not profit. Moreover, some matters in it will not be pleasant to those men who attribute themselves with a fortitude that is contrary to that which I set forth, though I do not doubt that they carry an affection for the virtue and love those who excel in it. Therefore, I persuade myself that, for Your Honor's sake, even among those which otherwise would tread it under their feet, it shall find some favor.

    I beseech Your Honor, for these reasons mentioned, to accept this simple offering. I wish and pray that the most mighty, the author and giver of all good gifts, will so far increase in you that heroic spirit of fortitude that Your Honor may abound in all noble and worthy acts, to the praise of the most high God, to the good of his church, and to your own eternal honor.

Your Honor's most humble to command.
GEORGE GIFFORD

A Treatise of True Fortitude

In our language, the term "fortitude" is derived from the Latin word *fortitudo*, which signifies, in the larger sense, all manner of force and strength. More strictly it is used for that virtue indicating manhood or valiant courage. It can also refer to greatness of mind, for it enlarges the mind and makes it stronger. We say of one that is valiant that he is a man of great mind.

The vice that is contrary to this virtue is cowardliness. In Latin it is called *pusillanimitas*, meaning smallness, slenderness, and weakness of mind.

The Hebrews have many different names to express this one virtue, such as *haiil, coah, geburah, hezek, maamats,* and *gnoz,* yet they all indicate strength and prevailing and are often used in a more general sense than the term *fortitude* itself.

Fortitude carries the greatest and highest praise among men. All those men who have been admired for their fortitude throughout history have excelled in greatness of mind. Among the Romans in ancient times, the title *magnanimous* was the largest, the richest and the most royal robe of honor which they could put on any man. It was more than just a crown of gold upon his head. When the poet was giving the highest praise to Rome that existed, he did it by praising the great minds of her citizens as comparable to the heavens.

The Grecians called their chief valiant men *heroes*. They admired them so highly that they believed them to be half gods. So, when we come to the people of God and the children of Israel, we see what the holy Scriptures say about the mighty.

The mighty men in Hebrew are called *gibborim, gibbore haiil, ansche haiil, ben haiil, abbirim,* and a man of war is called *isch milhamah.* Many were praised for their worthy acts because they were *ansche haiil,* men of courage. We see a number of examples among the kings, the judges, and the captains of Israel, those men like Joshua, Gideon, Jephthah, Sampson, and David. In the days of King David (2 Sam. 23) the Lord himself required of all those who held a public office – whether judge or teacher – that they be valiant in mind. Why? Because the mighty oppress the weak. How shall a judge execute true judgement unless he is a man of valiant courage?

If a minister of the word through cowardliness fears the face of man, how shall he reprove sin, especially in persons of high estate? Tyrants seek to invade kingdoms with great force. How shall the man of war be able to meet them and look them in the face if he does not have the heart of a lion? And what an honor it is to those who fight the battles of the Lord against the enemies of God, in defense of the truth, the church, and commonwealth, that the king of glory himself comes down to be praised among them and together with them. For it is written that "the Lord is a man of war," (Exod. 15:3), and that "The Lord is mighty in battle," (Ps. 24:8). This is high praise of the mighty.

Perhaps some will say, why is this virtue praised and held in admiration above all other virtues? Why should it have the highest honor? I answer that the cause is apparent to those that behold and view her well, with all the pleasant and sweet fruits that she brings forth. She makes great, for she is most excellently great, spreading herself through the height, the depth, the length, and the breadth of all goodness, inasmuch as the mind of man can never retain or practice any good thing without her force and might. She is as the sinews and bones of strength, knitting together and supporting the whole body of virtues. She lifts the mind of man: for through weakness man's mind is overcome by evil and brought to slavery. So, through strength it overcomes and gains the victory and is advanced to freedom and dignity.

She is the main pillar that supports both church and commonwealth. She opens the mouth of the judge to pronounce a true sentence of judgment without dread or respect of persons. She removes all fear from the messenger of God and makes him bold, so he may faithfully utter his full message to all degrees of men, both high and low. She girds on the sword of the mighty warrior and leads him forth with boldness to fight the battles of the Lord, to repel the violence of the enemy and to save the lives of many thousands. In regard to these things, her glory is brighter than the clearest star that shines in the heavens. There are many ornaments – gold, pearls, and other precious jewels – that may adorn the body. But all of them are far inferior to the ornaments she uses to adorn the mind of man. Her jewels cannot be valued at any price.

This noble virtue is worth seeking after, therefore, and blessed is he that finds the way to climb up to her. She dwells on high, and is hard to come to, as it is with all godly things. Her fame causes many to seek after her, but only a few find her, because so many are enticed and deceived by a vice which has stolen her cloak in an attempt to be like her. These run as swift as the roe, but look how far they are removed from the pure virtue they seek. To remedy this mischief, and to direct those who seek her, the way is to be opened which leads to the one and away from the other, for many a man can learn to avoid the wrong and to choose the right course.

And now we come to it. Fortitude is both human and divine. As to the first, the Gentiles could, by the light of nature, see and describe fortitude. They also labored to attain human fortitude by the natural powers and faculties of the mind through human courage.

Then there is divine fortitude where the mind through faith in Christ puts on the grace and power of God and thereby becomes great and valiant. As it is written, "Be strong in the Lord, and in the power of his might. Put on the whole armor of God," (Eph. 6).

If we consider each of these, we find in the one the right way to ascend to the palace of this princely virtue, and in the other, the race men run to that vice which resembles her. Those who seek to obtain her as a spiritual gift from God, by faith in Christ through the new birth by which the mind is renewed and made free, take the right way. They shall possess her; they shall taste of her sweet fruits.

But those who endeavor by their own natural powers and faculties of their mind, through human courage, to become valiant, run the wrong way, and although they attain to an exceeding hardiness, yet it is no virtue, but rather a resolute or desperate boldness, being only a mere vice under the show or resemblance of virtue. They run in the way of the Gentiles and cannot climb any higher than they did.

There are those who say they do not desire to obtain this virtue as the Gentiles did but prefer to do it a different way. Among them are some of the most valiant and brave-minded men that ever lived. No men have performed greater or more noble acts than they did, for which they have been held in admiration and honored above all men and shall be to the world's end.

We can look at ancient times to find many great men like Phillip of Macedonia and his son Alexander the Great, Scipio and Hannibal, Caesar and Pompey. Was there nothing but a show of virtue in these men? Was their courage and hardiness nothing more than a vice? We should esteem them and others like Julius Caesar as worthy patterns for all warriors to imitate.

Indeed, it can hardly be shown that there have been more soldier-like men in the world than some of those we have named, if we respect their skill to guide an army, their courage and boldness of mind, and also their famous acts.

And yet, without a doubt, they did not have in them the virtue of true fortitude, which is a most pure virtue; they only had some show of it. And so likewise the fame and the glory which they have secured even to the world's end is but a vain glory, and shall vanish, and at the last it will lay in the dust.

For proof of this, we must first look at this unwavering principle that there is nothing pure in man by nature, but all are wholly depraved and corrupted. As it is written, "they are corrupt and become abominable, there is not one that does good, no not one," (Rom. 3). Our Savior compares himself to the vine, and Christian men to the branches, and says "as the branch can bear no fruit of itself, except it abide in the vine, no more can you except you abide in me. Without me you can do nothing," (John 15). Without the new birth of Christ, there is not so much as a pure thought in any man. The mind is held captive to vanity and sin. How then shall so godly and so pure a virtue be found in nature?

Moreover, for a more particular proof that none of the famous men among the heathen had this true fortitude, consider this. All the most valiant and famed men of the Gentiles were under one or another of the four monarchies, or great kingdoms, which are described in Daniel 7. These kingdoms are compared to four savage beasts, that is, the lion, the bear, the leopard, and a beast very terrible unlike the rest. What is represented here by the beasts? Is it the civil power? Or the manners of those that ruled?

We should not think that the Holy Ghost represented the civil power by these cruel beasts, for civil power, even of the heathen kings, is of God. So, what then is resembled by those savage and cruel beasts, but the manner in which they exercised their power? The pride, the vainglory, the covetousness, the selflove, the ambition, the fierce cruelty, the craft, the subtilty, and the greedy ravening of the kings and stout warriors who set up and maintained those kingdoms are represented by the nature of those beasts. They gloried in the virtue that they died for their country, and all their valiant courage arose from those beastly vices. This is the glory of their noble acts. This is the praise which the Holy Ghost attributes to their manhood, no matter how men speak of them.

What then, was their great courage? Was it not that their hardiness was the gift of God, even in the heathen? This is undoubtedly the answer, that as God in his high providence ordained the great monarchies or kingdoms. He also prepared the instruments that should erect and uphold them. He put that skill into the warriors, and that heroism into those who fought. By his almighty power and wisdom, he uses all manner of instruments to execute his will.

But now we must understand that as this courage in itself was his gift, so was it by them corrupted, depraved, and abused through their pride, vainglory, covetousness, ambition, cruelty, and other abominable lusts. For these vices all nourished and supported their courage.

For example, consider Tamburlaine the Scythian who overthrew Baiazethes the mighty emperor of the Turks around 1397. A more valiant and expert soldier than this Tamburlaine could not be found, and yet he was as cruel a tyrant as ever did breathe. Shall we say that he had true fortitude? We must not think it strange that courage can be depraved and turned from virtue to vice.

Consider the creation and fall both of men and angels, and here we can learn to decide this matter. The angels of apostasy were created very godly creatures, resplendent with heavenly wisdom and fortitude. But they sinned and were consequently cast down from their high estate. They did not lose their understanding in their fall, but they corrupted and depraved it and turned it from wisdom into deep craft and subtilty. We do not say the devils are wise, but they are certainly exceedingly crafty. They have not lost their might and courage, but they have wholly depraved it and turned it from fortitude into a most obstinate, rebellious, and horrible devilish boldness.

Then look upon man before the fall, who also received good gifts of understanding and wisdom. In addition to understanding, he had pure valiant courage. The light of his understanding was not utterly wiped out by his fall, but it was corrupted and turned from wisdom. His courage of mind and hardiness was not destroyed but defiled, and from noble fortitude it was turned into an obstinate, proud, and cruel stoutness.

If the courage of the Gentiles was depraved in this way and turned from virtue into vice, how can fortitude be rightly divided into human and divine? Fortitude is a virtue, not only in show but in deed also. And if the courage of the Gentiles is not a virtue, where is our human fortitude?

But I do not call that human fortitude which the Gentiles had. For they knew one thing and practiced another. They had the law of nature, which is that God made man in his own likeness, an excellent creature, full of understanding and purity. He had the whole law written in his heart, so that he did not need to learn any knowledge of God from any other book.

This law was not quite blotted out by the fall, but remained in some part, as Paul speaking of the heathen, says, "that which may be known of God was manifest in them, for by beholding the frame of the world, his eternal power and Godhead are seen," (Rom. 1:19-20). The knowledge of good and evil remains in them, as the same apostle says, "the law is written in their hearts," (Rom. 2:15). And yet, Paul continues, "they did not glorify him as God, but withheld the truth in unrighteousness," (Rom. 1:18,21).

They also highly commended virtue and made many godly laws. This light in them is called the law of nature. By this they saw the deformity and uncleanness of vice but could not so much as have one pure thought to purge their mind from it. By this they saw after a sort the beauty of virtue, but they had no power with which to deck their hearts with it, not even so much as to think one clean thought. They could describe in some sort and commend fortitude, which is one branch of the law of nature, but they did not know the way to ascend up to her.

If this fortitude which the Gentiles defined could be a virtue indeed, and yet differ from the divine fortitude, then are there two fortitudes, and some will say that would be absurd. Are there two kinds of purity, or two kinds of virtues? If not, how could there be two kinds of fortitudes? I answer that fortitude being simply considered in herself is but one. But in regard to that estate we are in, the way by which we come to it, and the means by which it is given to us, it may well be called double.

Do not let it seem strange that a thing which is simple in itself may in some respects become double. For we know there is but one righteousness, being simply considered. And yet the holy apostle says that there is the righteousness of the law and the righteousness of faith, and sets them as opposite the one to the other. The righteousness of faith is the same purity which the law requires, as the same apostle teaches when he says that by Christ the righteousness of the law is fulfilled in us (Rom. 8:4). The law requires it, if only men could of themselves fulfill it (as Adam and Eve did before their fall). It might well be called the righteousness of the law, but now because man cannot fulfill it, being held under the yoke of sin, we obtain it only by faith in Christ who is made to us of God, wisdom, righteousness, sanctification, and redemption (1 Cor. 1:30). It is called the righteousness of God and the righteousness of faith.

So now regarding fortitude, the law requires it, and if men could by the natural powers and faculties of the mind attain to it, it might be called human fortitude. But because there is no such power in man, and the virtue can only come by a free gift in Christ, we may call it divine fortitude, and so the division of fortitude into human and divine is necessary to be known of all that desire to climb up to her.

Here may we see both the wrong way and the right. Those who labor to attain her by their own might have nothing with which to lift themselves up but human lust, because nature has nothing pure. They mount up on high with the wings of pride, vainglory, ambition, covetousness, and selflove. And there are some, who if they can attain to that desperate boldness as to become so resolute that they do not fear God nor man nor the devil, they think themselves to be brave men and are esteemed to be so. They do everything in the fierce wrath of man, which works nothing that is pure.

On the contrary, those that take the right way are cast down in humility, meekness, fear, and longsuffering. They are emptied of the opinion of all things in nature, which seem excellent in man, and whereby men are usually full of pride that they may be filled with gifts and graces from God. They mount up to a high state, but it is not in the strength of man. Rather, it is by the power and grace of God.

As that noble King David glories that the Lord made him strong and valiant, yes, so valiant so as not to be afraid of what man could do to him. He told that huge giant Goliath that he was coming to him in the name of the Lord, and in that name, he was able to cast him down and cut off his head.

As the Lord Jesus said, "he that exalts himself, shall be abased, and he that humbles himself shall be exalted." How contrary it is to man's wisdom, or to the sense of flesh and blood, that the right and only way to fortitude should be in lowlines of mind, in meekness, and in longsuffering. He seems valiant that is haughty, stout, fierce, and full of revenge, that does all with sturdy and boisterous roughness. But of these things we shall have occasion to speak more particularly in handling the nature of fortitude, which now we come to.

A perfect definition puts forth the whole nature of everything defined, for it includes the essential causes. But such definitions are hard to find in most things, and so to define fortitude is difficult. May it suffice to set forth some of its chief properties and effects. And in addition, we will also visit some of those things which the Gentiles rightly taught concerning this virtue.

First, true fortitude is never void of honesty and justice, nor can it ever be separated from these. For how can that be a virtue which is dishonest, unjust, or impure? Loftiness of mind is not a virtue but a vice if it is void of uprightness, for fortitude is a virtue that fights for equity. If any man who is hardy and full of stout courage casts himself into peril, led there by his lust and not for the common profit, that is to a wrong end. His courage is an audacious boldness rather than fortitude. He would be driven by his lust, which would lead him to do great things to get praise and fame, riches, and dominion. For the heart of man lusts for such things as selflove, pride, and vain glory. The higher a man's mind was lifted up by these into hardy boldness, the further he was carried from virtue into humanity or savage cruelty that expels all humanity.

By the light of nature, the Gentiles acknowledge that the things which outwardly seem beautiful, admirable, and glorious (as the acts of virtuous men), are foul, deformed, and detestable if they spring from the lust of man. For how can the fruit be sweet that comes from a bitter root? And what is more bitter then pride, ambition, selflove, covetousness, wrath, and such like?

Let us now rise higher than the Gentiles did, concerning the final cause of the actions of fortitude. Those will possess magnanimity who refer all to the common good and to be joined with simplicity and love of the truth. God made all for his own glory, which means that all actions are to be referred to his glory which is their chief and proper end, and that all the glory of man is in glorifying the great God.

He that is humble and lowly in his own eyes, not seeking praise and glory to himself which is vain, but delighting in the glory of God to perform great and noble acts by which that glory may be advanced, does not shun perils or refuse hard work. And in this is the true fortitude, the great mind. There is the man worthy of all admiration. He respects the maintenance of the truth and pure worship of God. He tends to the church; he seeks the good of the commonwealth and forgets himself.

Here are the sweet and pleasant fruits which spring from good roots, even from a sound virtue. By this it is evident, that the final cause gives the essential form to fortitude and makes her fruits wholesome. No man can climb up this high but through grace, even by the new birth in Christ Jesus. Because of itself, the mind of man is wholly overspread with vanity, and lusts after vain things, and cannot so much as have one motion towards a right end.

Now let us deal a little with those men which hold this perverse opinion, that a man cannot be both godly and valiant. They plainly perceive that the pure word of God requires humility, meekness, patience, gentleness, and longsuffering, and that without these no man can be godly. They do not believe these to be warlike properties, nor fit in any respect for a soldier. So, they suggest that the man who will study the word of God to follow and to practice it be chained up in the church like some fool, for he shall not be fit to deal in the affairs of the commonwealth. What kind of warrior shall he prove to be? And if a man is as proud as Lucifer, swearing horrible oaths, committing whoredoms, and living in other abominable vices, having cast off all fear of God like a devil incarnate that is fierce and stout to quarrel with bloody revenge, this is the man they extol above the clouds. He is the one whom they say has a brave mind; he is fit to make a valiant soldier.

This wicked error (if I may give it so soft a phrase) is not worthy to have an answer because they that hold it have, like monsters, killed the very light of nature so that the principles which the Gentiles held confuse them. For by those sparks of light which remain in nature, the Gentiles affirm that a virtue can never be void of that which is good, holy, and pure. For what is virtue but purity, holiness, and goodness? Those Gentiles conclude that no man can be both ungodly and imbued with fortitude. For how could the most pure and princely virtue be seated in a wicked impure mind?

Mark then how contrary this is to the speeches of our men, which say that fortitude and godliness cannot be joined together: and that a man cannot be both godly and valiant. What is this, as I said, but utterly to quench the light of nature, and to turn virtue into vice and vice into virtue?

And if brave-minded men are bold and yet ungodly, how is it that they have no sense of the true ornaments of the mind which deck it and make it brave? If a man is clothed in base, rotten, and ragged apparel, no man will say, "there goes a gallant fellow in fine attire," unless he speaks ironically. And if in addition to the baseness of his clothing he also stinks from filth, will any delight to stand near him with such an odor? The basest rotten rags or worst filth that can be found are not nearly so great a shame to the body as the lusts of the flesh like pride, ambition, covetousness, wrath, blasphemous, swearing, whoredom, etc.

And yet some will say that a brave mind may be clothed with these. They believe these to be sweet jewels that beautify. Otherwise, how could they say there is a brave mind, when it is defiled with them? This is the sense which they have of spiritual things. It is a beautiful, comely, and brave mind indeed that is decked with heavenly graces and virtues, including that of fortitude.

Some will reply that the mind which prevails may be called a brave mind, even for the courage and valor that is in it, although there is no godliness in it. I answer, then, whether base slavery may be accounted bravery? Take a man that has as much strength of body as three men who is a servile drudge, and his strength employed in the basest works that may be, as in emptying houses or cleaning filthy channels. Will any man recognize him as one who is living in freedom and bravery?

In the same way, where the mind is not set free from the yoke of vanity and corruption, it is employed in the service of human lusts. There is no baser bondage and drudgery. It cannot rightly be said that such a mind is in freedom, for it serves those foul stinking vices and is employed in their service. The Gentiles could say that he is the basest servant of all that is in bondage to his lusts. Solomon said, "I saw servants ride upon horses, and princes walking on the ground like servants," (Eccl. 10:7). He called those who have princely pomp in the world "servant" because they are still in bondage to their unclean lusts. And he called those men "princes" who have fortitude and freedom of mind to subdue and to reign over their inordinate affections and evil desires, although in the world they are of low estate.

It will be said further, where can it be shown, that such humble and meek men are proud valiant warriors? So, where are their noble acts? If men were well acquainted with the holy histories of the Bible, this question would not be asked. Abraham, the father of the faithful, was very valiant. With only a small company he pursued the great army of the kings and made a slaughter of them to deliver Lot, his brother's son, whom they had led away among the captives (Gen. 14). Joshua, a righteous godly man and the great captain over the children of Israel, fought great battles against many kings, and destroyed mighty nations, so the tribes of Israel could inherit the land that God had given them.

There were many valiant judges, holy men in Israel, which delivered them out of the hands of cruel and mighty tyrants. King David was a man after God's own heart, and yet the most valiant warrior that ever lived. Who can recount all his noble acts?

But why should I try to recount individuals? Read this one passage and you have your answer for all. For thus it is written, "And what shall I more say? for the time would fail me to tell of Gideon, and of Barak, and of Samson, and of Jephthah; of David also, and Samuel, and of the prophets, who through faith subdued kingdoms, wrought righteousness, obtained promises, stopped the mouths of lions, quenched the violence of fire, escaped the edge of the sword, out of weakness were made strong, waxed valiant in fight, turned to flight the armies of the aliens," (Heb. 11:32-34).

Let it be said then that a man who has no godliness at all in him can still be adventurous and accomplish great exploits and wars and defeat the enemy in defense of his prince and country. Should this man be respected and be seen as a brave-minded man? It is the good that comes by his valiant acts which is to be regarded, because he does as much good for his country as another. Sometimes it pleases God to use wicked instruments to work good to his people, but we must not take this as a general principle. For if we look well into the matter, we shall confess it to be otherwise.

Where do wars and bloody slaughters come from and what do they represent? It is widely known that they represent God's displeasure. God threatened to send his people a grievous plague, to be revenged upon horrible sinners. Then a godly great-minded man overthrew the enemies of God, with a blessing of peace which followed his victories, as the history of the judges of Israel shows through the examples of many godly kings. Wicked men also sometimes get victories, but not to finish wars, only to increase and continue them. Pouring on oil or throwing dry straw on a fire only causes it to burn higher. And since sins are the cause of wars and inflaming the wrath of God, ungodly warriors only serve to increase and continue them, and make them worse. For the chief captains are often irreligious, given to drunkenness, whoredom, and horrible swearing. It is amazing to see all the monstrous abominations which common soldiers commit. An army of them in a single month can be enough to pull down the wrath of God upon a whole kingdom. The most high is the protector both of the king and of the whole kingdom, and through his favor and blessing they stand and flourish. The king and the kingdom are not obligated to those men who live ungodly, though they do a great service for the commonwealth, because they provoke the wrath of God, and in so doing put the state of both the king and kingdom in jeopardy. For that reason, they are in more danger because these hardy warriors sin so grievously.

Let us not think, therefore, that the deeds of hardy men which are ungodly, are as good and beneficial to their prince and country as the noble acts of fortitude. They are neither brave-minded men nor good to their prince and country. In truth, fortitude and godliness cannot be separated. Only the godly man is brave-minded and profitable to his country, prince, and commonwealth, seeing ungodly warriors put their people in danger.

Now let's consider what the great and valiant mind says, two of which the Gentiles affirm. The one is in the despising of all external things; the other in doing great and difficult but profitable acts that include painful labor and extreme peril. The first is the cause that makes great men, and the other is the effect of their excellency. For the man who is so prepared mentally to dismiss all external things is fit to endure any travail and to pass through all perils and dangers, to do noble and famous acts. Once the former is obtained, the latter naturally follows.

The Gentiles believe that we should only desire and admire that which is worthy of man. And that nothing is worthy of man but virtue. They also taught that a man is to consider nothing as his own but the treasures of the mind. They believe the mind should be adorned with proper ornaments making her great, rich, and beautiful. So, if she retains these, the loss of all other things is nothing.

Further, they contended for such a lofty state and freedom of mind that is not subdued by man nor fortune, lust nor bondage. They aimed also at such a pleasant, sweet, and delectable calmness in which the mind should solace herself, being fully contented with the beauty and honor of those ornaments and rich jewels which are within her, that neither fear, grief, pleasure, nor wrath might disturb her. For thus they reasoned that such a mind content to delight in her happy treasures would not be disturbed or hindered by fear or grief, much less by lusts and pleasures of the flesh. For a man cannot delight both in unclean pleasures and in virtues.

The Gentiles could not see any higher, because their darkness was thick and deep, and their light was as a small candle. But we have the broad sunshine and clear light from heaven, by which we may see far higher. We find that we are utterly empty and void in ourselves of all good things. Our minds are not only robbed and spoiled of all goodly jewels and ornaments, but also are full of foul deformities and miserable bondage. There is no glorying in ourselves. We cannot stand on our own bravery. But here is the groundwork of all fortitude. The most high God is the fountain of all good things. He offered himself to us in his son, to redeem us out of our bondage, to make us his sons, and to become our inheritance. The mind that through faith embraces these promises and possesses him, possesses all heavenly treasures, riches, beauty, honor, glory, freedom, life and joy – all goodly ornaments to deck herself with. This is where greatness and valor come from, which is those heavenly and spiritual things we have in God. All external and transitory things here below are base, beggarly, and vile. For what is comparable to the God of glory, or what is equal to the happy life or joy in him?

Upon this therefore we are to stand and to make more particular discourse, in order to see how we can ascend up to this virtue.

Those external things which are despised by the noble valiant mind are many, yes, as many as all things under the sun. But we may categorize them as things prosperous, or adverse, pleasant or unpleasant, good or evil. For some of the philosophers used to divide goods into three kinds, as the goods of the mind, the goods of the body, and the goods of fortune.

The first are virtues or treasures of the mind. The second are health, strength, comeliness, and such which may be identified as riches of the body. The third is wealth, honor, fame, dignities, friends, and all of that sort. These are the goods of fortune. Then by default, there are three categories of similar evils answerable to these, as vices against virtues: sickness, feebleness, and deformities against the good things of the body; poverty, dishonor, contempt, infamy, reproach and enmity are all opposite to those goods of fortune. Further, we can add carnal pleasures, delights, sorrows, fear, grief, and torments, which seem to touch both mind and body.

Now let's consider each of these three categories in particular, beginning with the third group. Riches, honor, fame and friends are all gifts of God, and of great benefit to man not only for this present life, but also if he is a godly man, to the furtherance of his salvation and increase of his glory in the world to come, for these may enable him to do many great good works and highly advance the glory of God. But now, when the godly mind respects the heavenly treasures of righteousness, of life and joy, with the freedom, glory and honor of the sons of God, she considers all the highest and greatest treasures and glory under the sun to be nothing but dross and vanity. Others have them in admiration, because they neither feel nor see anything greater than this great free mind which possesses glory and riches and despises these earthly goods as things transitory.

If she has them, she does not proudly glory in them. If they are taken from her, and in their place she experiences poverty, dishonor, infamy, and reproach, she is not broken nor dismayed, seeing as she has lost only the dross and retains her crown of gold which none can take from her. For nothing can separate her from God. Poverty, afflictions, and torments may be grievous, but she knows they are only momentary, and not worthy of the glory which shall be revealed. Health, strength, and comeliness are good things, but nothing when compared to the health, strength, and beauty which she has in God. Pleasures and delights of the flesh are sweet and delectable to the natural man. But to her that feels the joys of God, they are nothing more than swill and dross. She will not sell those true lasting joys for these vanishing delights. This is how fortitude advances the mind to such freedom, dignity, and greatness, such that her head is lifted up above all things in the world. Fear, sorrows, joys, and pleasures come all under her feet.

It will be objected by many that no one has ever attained such spiritual strength that they are completely dead to the world and despise all that is in it. It is true that the knowledge of God is not perfect in any. The faith is not perfect, and so the contempt of all external things by which fortitude speaks must also be imperfect. For according to the measure of the one is the other. If there could be in any the fullness of faith, there should be also the perfection of fortitude. It follows therefore that as all faithful men are imbued with this virtue, so some are weaker in it, and some stronger. Increase in lively faith and assurance of God's love, increase in contempt and despising all the high things of this world, and so increase in fortitude.

Again, we must know, that the perfection of fortitude is not in abolishing all human affections of grief, of fear, and such like, which is stoical, but in ruling over them. See how contrary the true divine fortitude is to the human fury which is in men. For as that grows from the despising of all outward things, so this is set at work through the love of them. For what causes many to rush into all dangers but the hope that they will thereby gain riches, honors, fame, and dignity to live in earthly pleasures. Would they so put their lives at risk if they should not be honored and praised of men for doing so? Would they take such pains if there were not some earthly benefit? Are they led with the love of God's truth and glory or care of the common profit?

To proceed further, we can consider examples of many worthy men who have despised the riches, the glory, and the pleasures of this world, and so were valiant, and performed exceedingly great and noble acts. It shall be enough to speak only of two: Moses and Paul.

Moses was borne in the time of affliction, when the king of Egypt had commanded that all the male children of the Israelites should be drowned. The daughter of Pharaoh found him and adopted him as her son. He was brought up in the court like a king's son in all honor and delights. The riches and glory of Egypt were his. And yet, in order to be the deliverer of his brethren as God raised him up to be, and in order that he might be fit to do mighty acts, his mind became great by despising all worldly wealth, pleasures, and glory. For it is reported of him, "by faith Moses when he was great, refused to be called the son of Pharaoh's daughter, choosing rather to suffer adversity with the people of God than to enjoy the pleasures of sin for a season. Esteeming the rebuke of Christ greater riches than the treasures of Egypt, for he had respect to the recompence of the reward. By faith he forsook Egypt not fearing the fierceness of the king, for he endured, as if he had seen him which is invisible," (Heb. 11:24-27). May we see here how with mighty courage of mind, he disregarded all things in the world, which others do admire. And in so doing he became a mighty man, able to do great works both for the deliverance of God's people and also in conducting and governing them. Moses is one of the greatest examples of fortitude that ever lived.

Then considering Paul, what invincible courage he ascended to! What noble acts he abounded in! Let us see how he became fit for such great matters, so that he could pass through all labors and perils, because his mind was also lifted up and made free, great and mighty.

He despised all transitory things, no matter how they glittered to the outward eye and no matter how admired they were by worldly men. Read what is written of him and see how he said that the world was crucified to him, and he to the world. The most high was his inheritance. He did not fear death nor any danger, but passed through all hard things to serve God, to advance his glory, and to bring men out of destruction to life.

To recount all would be too tedious. It shall be enough to look at one testimony which he is forced to give of himself when the false apostles sought to discredit his ministry. "Are they Hebrews? So am I. Are they Israelites? So am I. Are they the seed of Abraham? So am I. Are they ministers of Christ? (I speak as a fool) I am more; in labors more abundant, in stripes above measure, in prisons more frequent, in deaths often. Of the Jews five times received I forty stripes save one. Thrice was I beaten with rods, once was I stoned, thrice I suffered shipwreck, a night and a day I have been in the deep. In journeyings often, in perils of waters, in perils of robbers, in perils by mine own countrymen, in perils by the heathen, in perils in the city, in perils in the wilderness, in perils in the sea, in perils among false brethren, in weariness and painfulness, in watchings often, in hunger and thirst, in fastings often, in cold and nakedness..." (2 Cor. 11). The martyrs in all ages, not only men but women also, have demonstrated their invincible fortitude by despising all the tortures and torments which bloody tyrants could put them through.

Now we see from what root this noble virtue springs, where her greatest victories and conquests consist, and what strong enemies she vanquishes. For in this it may be more apparent that these are those who can be counted among the great, brave-minded men. It is a most sure principle that fortitude eliminates all adversaries. He that overcomes the weaker, is he the man with the great mind? Is there found the praise and glory of fortitude? Then seeing it is so, that fortitude cannot be vanquished by any adversity whatsoever, but is able to overcome all, he is the great man with a valiant mind which conquers not only the lesser and weaker, but also the greater and the stronger.

Then it may be said, which is the weaker, and which is the stronger? I answer that men are the weaker. Men are but flesh and blood, even the strongest and the mightiest that ever lived are still weak in comparison to the devils, which are principalities and powers and rulers of the darkness of this world. Also, what is an army of flesh and bones when compared to the things in the world, such as "the lust of the flesh, the lust of the eyes, and the pride of life," (1 John 2:16).

So, then he that conquers men, and yet is conquered by the devil and by his own lusts and pleasures, is he great, is he strong? Is he free? Is he the noble-minded man? How absurd a thing it is to think so! If he can vanquish those like Alexander and Caesar of the weaker, which are men like himself, and yet be led away captive of the mightier, how is he the better? He then is strong and mighty, which overcomes not only men, but devils and wicked lusts. All this Paul sets forth in Ephesians 6.

The devil is our great enemy, working in the corrupt lusts which are in man's heart. He takes hold by pride, by vainglory, by ambition, by selflove, by covetousness, by wrath, and by unclean lusts and pleasures, to subdue and lead the mind captive to eternal slavery.

It follows that if through fortitude a man would break the cords and chains by which the devil leads him captive, he must begin with himself, even as a mighty prince subduing his own affections. This is it which the Holy Ghost has spoken by Solomon, "he which is slow to wrath is better than the mighty, and he that rules over his own spirit is better than he that wins a city," (Prov. 16:32). The Gentiles were not ignorant of this, for they affirm that he cannot be great who is in bondage to his lusts.

The man who is able to conquer himself is stronger than the warrior that defends a city. It is apparent then, by the light of nature, that the strongest fortresses and the highest walls for this noble fortitude to scale and win are in a man's own mind. There are the forts and munitions, there are the high things which exalt themselves against God, as Paul teaches in 2 Corinthians 10. Here is the labor, this is the work, here is the great glory of fortitude.

I might refrain from speaking any further of conquering the devil and man's own lusts, but that there is an incurable error in many men concerning manhood, as it consists in private revenge. If a man is challenged with some reproachful term, as to be called "coward" or "boy," and does not seek revenge, they conclude that he is utterly dishonored, and that the glory of his manhood is stained forever. Some protest this as glorying in manhood, that if such reproach should be offered them, they will be revenged, and kill or be killed, choosing rather to die with honor than to live with dishonor.

To answer these, we are sure that fortitude or an honorable manhood is a virtue most commendable when joined with wisdom, which brings forth sweet and pleasant fruits that highly honor God and are very good and profitable to men. We are also as sure on the contrary, that this kind of manhood (if I may call it that) which prides itself in private quarrel and bloody revenge, springs from the lusts of man and from wrath, vain glory, and disdainful pride.

The devil plays a big part in this kind of anger, as it is written, "be angry but sin not, let not the sun go down upon your wrath, neither give place to the devil," (Eph. 4). And Solomon says that "anger rests in the bosom of fools," (Eccl. 7:9). God says, "avenge not yourselves nor give place to wrath, for vengeance is mine, says the Lord, and I will repay," (Rom. 12:19). Anger takes the sword out of the hand of the prince, who is the minister of God to take vengeance on the evil doers (Rom. 3). The fruits which it brings forth are quarrelling, railing, horrible swearing, and cruel murders. This is the glory of their manhood.

Rather, those who by the mighty power and grace of God have subdued their corrupt lusts, so that they are meek, lowly, and longsuffering, and would rather suffer injury and bear reproach than disobey the truth, have attained great fortitude. But those who like to show their courage in private quarrels do not deserve to be called valiant or brave men, but quarrelers, hackers, and murderers.

Some will smile and say the meek make their conscience a covering for their cowardliness. When a man has no manhood in him, he pretends to be humble, patient, and longsuffering. How shall it be known what is in a man if he will not fight? To answer this, I say that if a man is withheld from revenging himself through cowardliness of heart, it is no virtue. But if he is one that will not in a right quarrel fear any man, then he is not making his conscience a covering for his cowardliness.

And concerning his valor, has fortitude no way to manifest herself, but by quarreling? No, the man who, for the defense of truth and of prince and state, shows himself as a mighty lion against the enemies of God, and in peace, or concerning private quarrel is lowly, gentle, courteous, and meek as a lamb, he is the great man indeed. He shows himself valiant in every way. He is to be honored, loved, and admired of all men. His fruits are delectable. As for the other, those fierce quarrelers, they are very dangerous and unprofitable. They are not to be commended but disallowed and dispraised, as those that would turn virtue into vice, and vice into virtue.

As there is great difference between him that is valiant through virtue, and that man which is hard and bold in the pride and lusts of corrupt flesh, so is there a great difference between their honor and reward for their acts. The hardy man according to the flesh seeks praise among men and has it. But what is that? Even a puff of smoke that vanishes with the breath of men's mouths. He seeks riches and finds them. But riches shall not deliver in the day of vengeance. He seeks pleasures of the flesh and swims in them. He takes delight and solace in fulfilling the sinful lusts of his flesh, but these pleasures of sin last only for a while, and endless sorrows follow. Their glory shall be turned into shame.

If only for a thousand years, even for a thousand thousand, if they could have some relief from their pain it would be some source of comfort. But when an infinite number of years are passed, they continued to be tormented because that which is infinite cannot be diminished. The sands of the sea are innumerable, and if every thousand years a bird picks up only one grain and carries it away, she shall take all away before their sorrows end.

The godly valiant man seeks the praise and glory of God. And "he that honors me," says the Lord, "I will honor," (1 Sam. 2:30). His glory is great with God and shall stand for ever. He covets the riches and joys of heaven, and he shall possess them forever, even world without end. His state shall never fail.

Therefore, you men of courage and hardy boldness, seek to have your courage sanctified and applied to the right use. Do not let it be lifted up with the wings of human lusts, to seek after vanity, but be strong in the Lord, not only to vanquish men which are weak, but to subdue the devils and your own corrupt affections, that your great mind may with heroical courage lift up her head above all enemies and enjoy that blessed freedom and dignity, that you may be great princes forever. For all conquerors shall be crowned with glory and immortality.

FINIS.

A Sermon on Psalm 133[13]

To the Worshipful Master William Rider, Alderman and Elect Sheriff of London.

Sir, this sermon was preached at St. Paul's Cross the 30th day of last May. At the time, there were some in attendance that put down the same in writing as nearly as they could remember. But when their copies were collected and compared, they were found to be incomplete. For this reason they made request that the preacher record the same as nearly as his memory would allow him. This I have done, and by public authority have gotten it printed so it could be distributed, I hope to the good of many. And finding myself greatly indebted to Your Worship and yours for your many courtesies, I was bold to present to you a testimony of my thankfulness, hoping that you will accept the same in as good a spirit as I meant it. And so beseeching God to bless Your Worship to the fulfilling of that hope, I humbly take my leave this 7th day of August 1591.

Your Worship's humbly affectionate to command.
T. C.

---

[13] A Sermon preached at St. Paul's Cross the 30th day of May, 1591. By M. George Gifford, Preacher of the word of God at Maldon in Essex. (London: I. Windet, 1591).

"Behold, how good and how pleasant it is for brethren to dwell together in unity!" (Psalm 133:1).

The holy prophet, King David, was the composer and writer of this Psalm, as the title expressly mentions. It is called a song of degrees, as there are 14 others besides this, set together under the same title, but in what sense? The learned interpreters are of diverse judgments, so I will adhere to what is most probable by the holy Scriptures.

The word *mahalaw*, which the prophet uses here, signifies steps or stairs by which we ascend into higher places. But by metaphor (as I take it to be used here) it signifies high estate, high degree, excellency, or dignity. For proof of this, we look at 1 Chronicles 17:17, where David, speaking to God, says, "thou hast regarded me according to the estate of a man of high degree." This is the same word used here. And if we consider that in the Hebrew tongue, to indicate the superlative degree they use the plural number, "a song of degrees," that is, "a song of excellencies," or "a song of dignities" is the same as saying "a most excellent" or "a most worthy song." In giving this title, the Holy Spirit is setting a mark in the forehead of this Psalm to give notice to us that there is a treasure of most excellent doctrine, and most fit for our instruction contained in it, and so we must give greater diligence and attention to it.

The argument or the matter here handled is singular. For the Holy Spirit with a very high and singular praise, through the whole Psalm puts forward and commends the unity and concord of brethren. The brethren to whom he is speaking and who are to keep this holy agreement are all the faithful children of the Church, fellow members of the mystical body and true worshippers of God, among whom is the spiritual brotherhood.

The virtue itself which is here commended is that same virtue which Paul so earnestly exhorts and persuades all Christian men toward, which is to keep the "unity of the spirit, in the bond of peace," (Eph. 4:3). The primitive church is commended for this practice, in which we have a lively example set before us. For it is written, that the multitude of them were of one heart and of one soul (Acts 4:32). For as one body consisting of many members has but one heart and one soul by which all the members are united and love each other, so the multitude were united in judgment and affection, as if there were but one heart and one soul in them all.

The commendation and praise by which the Holy Spirit sets forth the excellent worthiness of this virtue is under two Epithets, which are these: good and comely. For he said, "behold how good and how comely a thing it is, for brethren also to dwell in unity." These two Epithets he afterward opens and amplifies by two examples: one is taken from the anointing of Aaron with precious ointment to declare the sweet and pleasant comeliness of this unity, and the other is taken from the dew of Hermon, which comes down upon the mountains of Sion to produce the fruit and good that comes from it.

And finally, he concludes with the highest cause, the Lord God, who commanded the blessing of life eternal to be upon this unity. This is a brief summation of the Psalm, or of this praise which is given. Now let us come to the exposition.

Beginning with the first word, the prophet stirs up the minds of the Israelites, even of all the tribes, to realize how blessed a thing unity and concord is. They know this by their own experience. For in former days they had had much sorrow, great calamities, harms, and annoyances of discord; and at this present time when this Psalm was given, they saw the blessings and benefits of unity and peace. For their former experience in the days of King Saul, when he persecuted David who had done no evil, the worship of God was neglected. Good men were oppressed, and evil men flourished. There was much discord, to the grief of many. Then when Saul was taken away, and David was anointed king in Hebron, Abner, the son of the captain of Saul's army, took Ishbosheth, Saul's son, and set him up to be king. When this happened, the discord among the tribes grew much greater, for then one part of the tribes sided with David, the other with the house of Saul. They were indeed all the sons of Jacob and professed the God of Abraham, whom they should with one mouth have worshipped and glorified as Paul said in Romans 15:6. But they were divided, and bloody wars broke out between them that continued for a long time among the tribes (2 Sam. 2:2-3). Brethren with deadly hatred and enmity pursuing their brethren, seeking the blood of each other. In this time of discord great calamities spread throughout the whole land. They saw firsthand how mischievous a thing it is for brethren to be at odds.

The cutting down of so great an evil and the removal of all its remnants is a very great good. Therefore, when Abner and Ishbosheth were slain, all Israel came together and set David up as king. Tribes were reconciled to each other, and those who rent each other asunder again became one body. Brethren embraced each other with love, the bitter hatred that existed before among them was cut down and extinguished. The worship of God was now set up, the blessings of God were powered down from heaven upon them in great measure, and the whole land rejoiced with joy and gladness. Now he wants them to behold how good and how comely a thing it is for brethren to dwell at unity. They were taught this by their own experience on both sides, for they had known the grievous annoyances of discord and enmity on the one hand, and the benefit of peace on the other. This is why he urges them to "behold how good and how comely a thing it is, which cuts down such a great evil, and behold how good and how comely a thing it is that brings with it such great blessings of God."

Now to the praise itself: the first Epithet contains the fruit that arises from the first and is afterward set forth by the second comparison, that is, of the dew of Hermon. For that is a thing fruitful and good. The other is the word is *magnim*, which signifies beauty, sweetness, comeliness, or pleasantness, as in Psalm 16 where he speaks of the resurrection and exaltation of our savior Christ, saying, "Thou wilt show me the path of life, in thy presence is fullness of joy, and at thy right hand there are pleasures for evermore." This comely pleasant sweetness of concord is represented by the former example, that is, of Aaron's anointing, for that was a very comely and a sweet thing and had a mystical significance.

To understand better what is meant here, you may first read of this precious ointment, both that the Lord commanded to be made, and how Aaron and his sons should be anointed with it into the office of the priest, in Exodus 30. Further, we are taught in the Scriptures that Aaron was a figure of Christ, and that Aaron's anointing with that precious sweet ointment represented the spiritual and heavenly anointing of Christ Jesus with the Holy Ghost, whose graces distill from his head to every part of his mystical body, which is the Church. Of him it is said, "the spirit of the Lord is upon me, because he has anointed me," (Luke 4:18). Mark further where this comparison holds. Pouring the precious ointment on Aaron's head, watching it run down his head to his beard and drop onto his clothing was pleasant to behold and put out a sweet aroma to all who stood around. Also, in that it descended down his beard and onto his clothing, it resembled the graces of the Holy Ghost flowing down from the Lord Jesus Christ upon all the members of his body knit together in holy unity. The oil trickled down from Aaron's head to his body and onto the lowest part of his garment because there was no rent or separation between them.

Even so the Church united in Christ, her head, and every member of the same united with the rest in a holy union, making all one body, the heavenly graces of the Holy Ghost being far sweeter than that precious ointment, flowed from him upon them all, as all are partakers, even to the lowest and meanest member. For where they are joined in this spiritual unity, look what graces God from his Son Christ pours upon the highest members (that is, upon princes and pastors), and then they distill also upon the other parts and members, from each to each other.

That which was separate from the head, from the body, and from the garments of Aaron received none of that precious ointment which descended from the head to the body which was united with it, and to all parts of the garments sewn together. In like manner the graces of the Holy Ghost descend from Christ the head upon nothing that is separate and divided from him, but upon all the members united in one body.

We may now briefly establish what this example declares in this passage. The sweet ointment is poured over the head of Aaron, it flows down to his beard, then upon his shoulders and all parts of his body even to the lowest border of his garments. Jesus Christ, the head of the Church, is anointed with the Holy Ghost, and from him the sweet graces descend over the whole body and upon every member of the body even to the lowest, this is what it means to be united to him and to his Church; this is a thing most sweet and most comforting.

In the other example, he resembles this unity of the dew of Hermon, which comes down upon the mountains of Sion, the waters which fall upon the high mountains distill into the valleys which are joined at the foot of the mountains, to make them plenteously fruitful. Even so, the heavenly spiritual dews come down from above upon the mountains, flow through the valleys which are united there to produce great fruit. There is much for us to consider in these examples, which express how good and how comely a thing it is for brethren also to dwell in unity.

Now all this is from the most high God, that those who dwell together in this holy unity, the Lord has commanded to bless with life forevermore. It is God's unchangeable decree that they shall receive the blessing of all blessings in everlasting continuance. This can never fail, for God almighty is unchangeable, and what he decrees and commands shall stand forever. This may persuade many to dwell in unity, for it is good to be under the blessing of almighty God. And he has commended his blessing on the unity of the brethren and there only.

Now that we have seen the praise of unity and concord here set forth, it remains for us to consider to what end and purpose the Holy Ghost gives this great commendation. This we all know, that when a thing is spoken of negatively, it is to bring us to a shunning of the same, as a thing either unpleasant or hurtful. Contrariwise, praise, especially where it is given by God who knows the worth of everything, is to cause us to love that which is praised. This is done here, that we may have our hearts inflamed, and that we may be in love with unity and concord, and that we may studiously seek after it and embrace it as a most precious jewel.
Finally, take heed that we do nothing which may hinder and disturb the same. And if this cannot move us, and kindle an earnest love and zeal to be studious of godly peace because it is good, sweet, and pleasant, and God's blessing is upon it unto eternal life, how dull are we to spiritual and heavenly things, or what can move us? Shall we not care to have that cut down which brings mischief and destruction, and to set up that which carries all blessedness with it? Shall we neither care to avoid the curse of God, plagues, and punishments on the one hand, and not covet to have his blessing on the other? I will come now to the application of this Psalm to our estate.

We have, as you all know, received great blessings from the Lord our God by the means of our gracious Queen. For by her happy reign, we have long enjoyed peace, such as has never before been seen or heard of in this land. We have also enjoyed a bounty of all things, our country overflowing with milk and honey, every man sitting under his vine and under his fig tree. And moreover, the Lord has protected us by her scepter and power, from the invasion of foreign enemies and from the wicked practices and treasons of domestic adversaries. These are great benefits indeed. But the greatest blessing of all is that by her government, he has delivered us from the bondage of Pharaoh, from the heavy yoke of antichrist, out of idolatry and blindness, and has restored to us his holy word and true worship.

Notwithstanding there have been among us, for many years (as you all know) great discord among not only papists and other enemies of holy religion, but even among brethren which profess the same holy doctrine and faith of our Lord Jesus Christ. All this time we have tasted the bitter fruits of enmity and discord, we have felt and sustained the mischiefs, harms, and damages that grow from it, so that we have had experience with the Israelites in the worser part, and can say of our own knowledge, behold how evil and how uncomely a thing it is for brethren to be at odds. To make this more apparent, if I could lay open all the evils which have already come upon us by the discord of brethren, it would be a long and tedious labor. I will therefore only note some of the chief and most general, those that have been our most grievous wounds, that we may seek to have them cured if it pleases God.

First therefore, I may note as a principal evil fruit of enmity, that it is a joy to the enemies of the Gospel to see brethren set against brethren. For as in an army of men, if they are at deadly opposition among themselves, captain against captain, band against band, pursuing each other, that their common enemy (against which they should wholly band together their forces) will say, we do not need to do much, for we shall easily prevail. They will pull down and destroy themselves with their own hands, and in this we will rejoice. So is it in God's Church, Christ's army, surrounded by deadly enemies on every side, when there is discord growing into sharp enmity, and the leaders themselves are bent one against another, the wicked enemy laughs, and receives boldness and strength. He says in his heart that this sharp contention among them will proceed in the end even to blood, and to the desolation of both parties. O! how much we ought to be grieved at the rejoicing and emboldening of God's enemies! And how woeful a calamity is this, if among brethren this enmity should come to blood?

As we saw among the children of Israel with the discord and enmity ended in the shedding of blood, unless the Lord in great mercy turns it away, the end among us will also be most grievous. This one evil ought to move us to love and embrace the holy unity here commended in this Psalm. I would that the consideration of it might be deeply printed in our minds.

The wounding of the weak is another great evil that arises from discord. Many are cast down, or turned out of the way, or at the least greatly hindered in our Church by discord when these stumbling blocks are laid before the blind and lame. With what pity this ought to move us, and how much the sight of it should vex and grieve us, as the doctrine of our Savior Christ uttered by himself and by his apostles show everywhere. Also, threatenings and woes are pronounced against them who cast down the weak. Shall we not regard this thing at all? Shall neither the compassion and love for our brethren for whom Christ died, nor the threatenings and woes denounced against us make any difference?

Thirdly, the discord of brethren brings both parts into contempt and spreads disgrace among many. And so, the ministers of the Gospel, the messengers of Christ who should be esteemed for their works' sake as vessels of gold and silver in the Lord's temple and as angels of the Lord of hosts, are basely esteemed as if they were vessels of earth and wood. If this contempt reached only to men themselves, it might be somewhat less grievous. But for the contempt to extend to the glorious Gospel of Jesus Christ, because in the disgrace of the men the power of their ministry is weakened, is intolerable indeed. For where the teacher is evil thought of and despised, the multitude does not regard his doctrine. This evil goes deep, and if we consider it together with what I have mentioned earlier, you will see that upon our own experience we may say, indeed, behold how evil and how uncomely a thing it is for brethren to be at enmity and discord. These evils highly displease almighty God, and if they continue without remedy, who can show the punishments and calamities that will, in time, come upon us in this land? The contempt of the Gospel, growing into atheism will draw down infinite plagues and miseries. For the righteous God will not always allow such abuse unrevenged.

Unity is so good, bringing so many blessings, and discord is so evil, drawing such a heap of mischiefs with it. The one is a nourisher of true life and should be sought after and maintained by all godly Christians, and the other should be despised as a deadly pestilence. This should be done of us speedily because dissention is like the breaking out of water. The longer it continues, the wider the breach that is made and so becomes the more difficult to be recovered. I think that no man will deny that it is a most necessary thing in God's church and among brethren, to avoid discord and to seek unity.

Therefore, let us now consider and understand how it is to be sought. Let it be that we both agree it is to be sought, and also that we seek for it. But if we do not seek it the right way, we are never the better for seeking it at all.

Know this first, that there are two sorts of unity and agreement, the one is in God, being in you truth, in the spirit, in true holiness and sanctification. The other is in error and sin and not in the Lord. Now indeed it is the holy unity in the Lord, which is praised in this Psalm, and which we must seek after, upon which the blessing of God shall come. You can see this in that exhortation of Paul in Ephesians 4:3 when he says, "make every effort to keep the unity of the spirit through the bond of peace." One of the reasons he adds this is because there is one body, and one spirit, and you are called into one hope of your calling: *one Lord, one faith, one baptism, one God and Father of all, etc.* For like as all the members of the natural body are coupled together by one soul and make up one body, so by one spirit of the Lord all the faithful are united and become all one mystical body of Jesus Christ. By one faith and one baptism, they are all in one Lord and in one God. The foundation of this unity is the truth, and by it men grow up together in God. For this cause it is said in the first verse of the Psalm, "Brethren are also to dwell in unity," because as there is a reconciliation wrought by Christ between God and man, so that man is come into unity with God, he must also grow into unity with those which are together reconciled to the Lord with him. Christians are to seek this unity, to be united with our brethren unto God; otherwise, we will be dissolved and scattered again in confusion.

  Regarding that other unity, which is in error and wickedness, those who possess it commend it. For example, the papists make a great proclamation against those of us who profess the glorious Gospel, saying we have disturbed and broken this holy unity by rending ourselves from the true Church, and so from the faith and from Christ's mystical body. However, this is a grievous accusation, because it is most evident that they have forsaken the truth of God. They blaspheme and condemn it, and set up abominable errors and cursed idolatry. The lot of them is nothing more than a most wicked and cursed conspiracy against God and his people. What, is their unity more than that which is described by the Prophet David in Psalm 2, "Why do the Gentiles rage, and the people meditate that which is vain? The Kings of the earth stand up, and the Princes take counsel together against the Lord, and against his Christ."

Herein is a great unity, or rather a conspiracy, of wicked traitors against Christ. This perplexity is fulfilled by them. And we have the commandment of God by the voice of the angel, "Come out from among them, my people and separate yourselves." All their proclamations are nothing against us because we have not dissolved this blessed unity here commended, but have forsaken their cursed conspiracy, of which the nearer a man is joined to, the further he is from God. Let no man therefore be troubled by their accusations, but forsake them, embrace the holy faith, and be united together with the prophets and apostles and all holy men, unto Jesus Christ.

You will hear many other kinds of men complain that there is no fellowship and unity kept with them.

Indeed, they walk after their wicked and unclean lusts and abominable sins, in contempt of God's word, and in drunkenness, whoredom, pride, ambition, covetousness, usury, extortion, bribery, oppression, envy, and many other similar sins. The Holy Ghost tells us to have no fellowship with these unfruitful works of darkness, but rather reprove them (Eph. 5:11). We cannot join Christ and Belial, we cannot be united to the Lord and have fellowship in wicked sins. If we say we have fellowship with God and walk in darkness, we lie (1 John 6, Eph. 5:11). He that cries out for peace, and yet walks in ungodly ways, straying from the truth and from sanctification, whatever he seems to be, he is nothing more than a disturber and breaker of all holy unity. For who can take part with him in those things, without separating himself from truth and godliness, without which there can be no blessed unity.

Peter calls our Lord Jesus Christ a "living stone," unto whom all the faithful also become as living stones, built up to become a spiritual house (1 Peter 2). If stones are not squared up and made smooth to sit on top of one another and join together, how will they grow into one building? If men are not framed in faith and godliness, how will they be united in the Lord? Indeed, there are imperfections both in doctrine and manners, for all the best hewn stones have some ruggedness remaining, so men must bear with one another in harmony, for charity covers a multitude of sins (1 Peter 4). For while this temple of God is in the world, the stones are not perfectly set together but the work is still in process. This temple is still being built, so we must beware of the downfall on that side also.

Because this blessed unity must be in God, in the truth, to be built up in Christ Jesus in true sanctification (for he that is in Christ is a new creature) and seeing all unity without this foundation will fall down as a rotten building, let the holy book of God be our ground. Let it be useful to cut down all controversies, and let men if they look for any part of the blessing here promised, yield all honor and glory to this sacred word. Let no man stand upon his own honor or reputation. If he has maintained anything awry, as soon as he is aware of the truth in the natter, he must yield and let the truth of God go before and lead the way. For this is the only way to grow into this holy unity. And let those who walk awry, forsake their evil ways, embrace the heavenly truth, and follow the rules of the Holy Scripture if they will be accounted students of peace and concord.

For when we join to the truth, both in faith and godliness of life, we are joined together in the Lord, and it shall be said, "behold how good and how comely a thing it is, for brethren also to dwell at unity." It shall be like that precious ointment upon the head of Aaron. The heavenly graces and gifts of the Holy Ghost shall come down upon us in plentiful measure and flow unto every member. We shall bring forth fruit unto God watered with heavenly dews. And we shall know that great and high blessing of God almighty unto eternal life.

Therefore, if it is not too late; if the sins of this land have provoked the Lord to displeasure, let all men lift up their hearts and cry unto the Lord, that we may be at unity (not in all manner of wicked vices, nor in errors) but in the Lord.

And now, who shall seek this unity? Who shall make effort to advance it? I answer that all positions of men, private persons, rulers and teachers, every one that will look for any part of God's blessing must make effort to advance it. Every man must look unto the heavenly truth of the holy religion, and embrace the same with all love and hearty affection. Every man ought to be zealous in spirit for the glory of Christ.

For if a man does not have the zeal of religion, he cannot be a good man, whether he is a ruler or a private man, though he seems to be always peaceable. But as the Lord said to the Angel of the Church of Laodicea (Rev. 3), "Because thou art neither hot nor cold, I will spew you out of my mouth." God rejects all such dull atheists and irreligious persons which are so earthly minded that they do not regard the heavenly graces offered in the Gospel. Let all men therefore stir up their hearts to be fervent in God's truth and let not godly zeal be quenched. Then further, we must join the practice of this holy word, as the Apostle James tells us, "be doers of the word and not hearers only, deceiving yourselves," (James 2:19). For the great disturbance of peace and the grievous breaches of unity, and all bitter dissentions, chiefly result from all sorts and degrees of men who do not walk in the rules which God has prescribed to them in his word. We must therefore come more carefully to this matter, that we may see how each man is to further this blessed unity.

I begin with the private person. There are rules prescribed in God's word for him to observe if he will be a true member of the Church and a seeker and preserver of this unity and so a partaker of God's blessing unto life everlasting. One rule concerns subjection and reverence to rulers and governors, both civil and ecclesiastical, for God commanded us to honor and obey them. "Submit yourselves to every ordinance of man for the Lord's sake: whether it be to the king, as supreme, or unto governors, as unto them that are sent by him for the punishment of evildoers, and for the praise of them that do well," (1 Peter 2:13-14). In Romans 13:1-7, Paul also writes regarding this obedience and subjection for conscience sake, of this reverence and honor to be rendered. And Hebrews 13:17 says, "Likewise obey them that have the oversight of you and submit yourselves, for they watch for your souls as they that must give account." The neglect and breach of this rule, even the denying of obedience, reverence, and honor unto the rulers, governors, and teachers, disturbs and overthrows the unity which is here praised.

So, if a man does not consciously perform this duty in obeying the holy doctrine of the Lord, what is he, other than an enemy of true unity, a dissolver of unity and peace? But what if rulers offend, pastors and governors fail and come short in some duties, and thereby seem unworthy to be regarded? I say if they do, they shall answer to God for it, but still private men are not discharged from this obedience and from rendering honor unto them, for it is to the authority and to God's ordinance that they do it, and not in respect of man.

God has not prescribed the duties of men which are to be done unto others under the condition that they do all they ought to do on their part, or that they are the kind of men they ought to be. But he has prescribed every man's duty absolutely. If another fails in his, he shall answer for it before God. But his failure does not allow you to depart from the rule which God gave you to obey. For you are tied in conscience to God to obey his will, not in regard to man or of your own benefit to do this or that. For by this doctrine of the blessed apostle we see that Christian subjects and faithful servants are commanded for their conscience's sake to God, to give honor to heathen princes and infidel masters (Rom. 13 and 1 Tim. 6:1).

From this express command in the word of God we observe that when governors do wrong, men are not at liberty to revile and reproach them, or to dishonor them with evil speech, seeing it is also written, "Thou shalt not curse the ruler of the people," (Exod. 22:28). But on the contrary, prayers and supplications are to be made unto God for rulers and teachers of the Lord's people. When they offend, it is with great hurt to the Church, and therefore men are to mourn for it and not to make themselves merry with reproaches. Let all evil speeches of disgrace then be turned into prayers, and the laughter into tears, for this shall be more pleasing unto God. For we who breach the rules of this doctrine, of submission, of reverence and honor due to governors, are guilty of breaching the unity of the brethren.

Another rule given by the apostle is this, that you "study to be quiet, and to do your own business, and to work with your own hands, as we commanded you," (1 Thess. 4:11). As God has distributed unto every man, and as the Lord has called every one (1 Cor. 7:17), God has ordained the several callings, he has given gifts of abilities to men to perform the things he requires of the same. He has also set the bounds and limits within which everyone is to keep himself, and to walk orderly, dealing with that which pertains to him. This is a holy thing and comely, a preserver of unity. But this doctrine of unity is very broken and as a result, great evil ensues. For there are many private persons who seem very religious, that seem to seek the holy unity, but leave the duties of their own places and callings and busy themselves wholly with those matters which do not belong to them. As if the matters of their trades and sciences were too base, or as if the care of their family were unimportant, they set these aside and neglect them, and take upon themselves anything that is amiss in the Church, as if God had set them to be overseers of the governors and teachers. Contrary to this rule given by Paul, they labor not with their hands, nor meddle quietly with their own business, but they bend all the powers of their mind to dispute and reason about government, and the duties of governors and teachers, wandering about, and seeking to persuade and draw others to their cause. They think this is doing God a high service. But who gave them power to dispense with this rule, that you study to be quiet, and to meddle with your own business, and to labor with your hands? Has God called them and set them about greater things, and freed them from these? Is it not the ordinance and will of our God that men shall instruct and guide their families in his ways?

    We should labor to take care that the children and servants may learn the holy doctrine and walk in it. But there are many who meddle deeply in public matters, and if they have two or three children and as many servants, they are left ignorant; no effort is taken to train them so that they may not go astray. Also, a man's own matters which Paul urged us to deal with are in providing earthly things necessary for his family. Paul said that if there were any that did not provide for his own, namely for those of his family, he denies the faith, and is worse than an infidel (1 Tim. 5:8). And so it is in other duties. Every man is to look to his own way, that he keeps himself upright before God, for in reprehending another that he finds fault with, he neglects his own calling. "Therefore, thou art inexcusable, O man, whosoever thou art that judges: for wherein thou judges another, thou condemn thyself; for thou that judges does the same things," (Rom. 2:1). In doing so, you leave that small charge committed to you undone. And let us make the comparison, is he not more worthy of blame that finds fault with the greater, and not in the lesser, when the greater is more difficult to be performed? It is harder to govern a whole kingdom, a city, or a flock than a little family, and more faults will appear. How unreasonable then is it that a man who does not guide his little family in the way that God requires should let go the sight of his own defects, and wholly give himself in speech to deprave the public guides. Be sorrowful for evil, follow the ways of the Lord, obey the rules of the word. Let all men regard this and keep their place and standing which God has set them in, and so walk in such a way that they may answer before the high Judge and give account how they have discharged their duties.

    Let us come now to the governors and guides of the Lord's people, and first to the pastors and shepherds which have the power and authority ecclesiastically. These are principal parties to procure and to preserve this blessed unity, as the end they are given of Christ. As Paul states, "And he gave some, apostles; and some, prophets; and some, evangelists; and some, pastors and teachers," to this end: "for the perfecting of the saints, for the work of the ministry, for the edifying of the body of Christ, until we all come in the unity of the faith, and of the knowledge of the Son of God, unto a perfect man, unto the measure of the stature of the fulness of Christ," (Eph. 4:11-13). This is their whole work and labor appointed them, even to build up Christ's body, the Temple of God, by framing and coupling together the living stones unto that unity of brethren, which is commended in this Psalm.

Now let us see the rules prescribed in God's word which they must observe to perform this holy work. "The elders which are among you I exhort, who am also an elder, and a witness of the sufferings of Christ, and also a partaker of the glory that shall be revealed, feed the flock of God which is among you, taking the oversight thereof, not by constraint, but willingly; not for filthy lucre, but of a ready mind," (1 Peter 5:1-2).

First the sheep of Christ are to have food, for their life depends on it. It is required therefore in all shepherds that answer their calling before God, to have the same affection in them which Christ had, who when he saw the multitude, had compassion on them because they were as sheep without a shepherd (Matt. 9:36). Pity and compassion for the straying sheep must move them to feed the flock, and love must constrain. For Christ said to Peter, "Simon, son of Jonas, do you love me more than these? Feed my sheep. Do you love me? Then feed my lambs. Do you love me? Feed my sheep." It is as if he is saying, if you love me, then do this for me.

Those who are in authority in the church, I humbly beseech for the Lord Jesus Christ's sake, to have compassion upon the flock, that the sheep may have their necessary food, even the bread of life plentifully broken before them, that they may be led into the green pastures and unto the fountains and streams of the living waters.

    Cry also to the Lord of the harvest, that he will pour down his spirit upon them, that in compassion there may be laborers sent forth. And on those who have accepted the charge, may they be compelled to do their duty, that those who are unable to feed, or those who walk in a wicked manner in life and conversation, may be removed. And those who are skillful to teach and who live a godly life, may be able to guide them both by doctrine and example. If this is not performed, how is true concord and unity sought? If the people are not instructed and led in the way of godliness, how shall they be framed and built together in one holy temple? If the shepherd is ungodly and lives wickedly, what peace, what vanity, or what agreement can those who fear God, have with him? And if there is a division between the sheep and the shepherd, where is the unity of brethren? May the flock of Christ be fed and guided by skillful godly men which teach sound doctrine and live a good example in life and conversation.

    And now concerning the care of the flock, not by constraint or for gain, but willingly and of a ready mind, not as lords over God's heritage, but as examples to the flock, I again beseech the pastors and governors for Christ's sake, to abound and to increase in all fatherly love towards the Lord's people without which this care cannot rightly be performed. Follow the example of

Paul, who performed his labor not of ambition or desire for gain, nor with roughness, but as he said, "we were gentle among you even as a nurse cherishes her children," (1 Thess. 2:7). The Lord complained of the pastors of Israel, "Woe be unto the shepherds of Israel, who feed themselves, should not the shepherds feed the flocks? You eat the fat, and you clothe yourselves with the wool, but you feed not the sheep: the weak have you not strengthened: the sick have you not healed, neither have you bound up the broken, nor brought again that which was driven away: neither have you sought that which was lost, but with violence, and with cruelty have you ruled them," (Ezekiel 34:2-4).

This was the state of the flock then and shall be even to the world's end: that among Christ's sheep some are strong, some are weak, some sick, some going astray. Yes, such are the frailties of all the faithful, but they are still the sheep of Christ, the Israel of God, and the shepherds of Israel are to look after them. Now I say, if shepherds do not exhibit a fatherly love to cover the multitude of sins of the sheep, if there is no tender compassion as the nurse towards the little babe, to heal the broken and sick, and to support the weak, to bring home those who stray, they shall despise the sheep as not worthy to be regarded. For the greater the frailties, the greater the compassion to be shown.

Violence and rigor are not fit characteristics for shepherds. For shall the shepherd take his staff and strike the young and tender lambs? Or shall he beat and bruise the weak and feeble sheep? What shall we say, are the sheep of Christ of less value? Many of them are weak and feeble in knowledge, many of them are young babes in terms of their spiritual power of sanctification. Many are wounded in conscience and troubled in spirit. Here is the place for the love, the care, the compassion, and labor of shepherds. O! you shepherds of Israel put on this love and compassion, and do not despise the sheep of Christ for their frailties. Do not rule them with violence and cruelty: but feed and support and heal them with all meekness and longsuffering. For if you cause them to walk stubbornly against you, they shall never be able with patience and meekness to go accomplish the work they are called to do. And if we think that it discharges the shepherd from their responsibility to be tender and loving toward the sheep when the sheep do not respect and reverence him, consider Moses and Paul, two great and notable servants of God, two special shepherds of the Lord's flock. Who is worthy to be compared with them? They have left an example to be followed. What great things Moses did for the people of Israel. And yet how often did they murmur against him, and were ready to stone him? How many times did they rebel against him? Yet his love was not quenched, his care did not fail, but his prayer continued to be most earnest to God to pardon them. He still esteemed them as the Lord's chosen people.

Behold also the exceedingly abundant love of Paul, who wished himself accursed from Christ, if his kinsmen the Jews which were obstinate, might be saved. How much greater was his love to the faithful, his kindred? And yet did the Church of Jerusalem scarcely think anything well of him all the time he lived? This is gathered by what he writes in Romans 15 where he first showed that it pleased those of Macedonia and Achaia to give to the poor saints in Jerusalem, and he went with them to see it delivered. He further urged them to be very earnest in prayer to God for him, that he might be delivered from the disobedience of Judea, and that his ministry towards Jerusalem might be accepted by the saints. Paul persuaded the churches of the Gentiles to make a liberal contribution to the Church at Jerusalem, so great was his care. Yet when he showed all this love and diligence towards them, they despised him so that he feared his ministry would not be accepted by them. What caused them to dislike him so? It seems from Acts 21:21 that the reason was because it was reported that he taught the Jews who were among the Gentiles to depart from Moses' teaching and not circumcise their children. And yet he still loved them dearly, calling them saints, regardless of their frailties in this matter and the hard opinion they held of him, so great and so worthy a servant of the Lord Jesus Christ. What a pattern of meekness and fatherly love is here for all the shepherds of the Lord's flock to follow, to care for the poor, feeble and wandering sheep who do not reverence and regard them as they should.

Peter states that shepherds must be examples to the flocks, and therefore all should demonstrate meekness, longsuffering, and that love which covers a multitude of sins. Where the pastors abound in this fatherly love, and do not harm the frail sheep and tender lambs with rigor and violence, the blessed unity of brethren here praised is chiefly furthered. The building up of Christ's body in sanctification is greatly advanced by the example of these pastors and teachers. The multitudes are drawn to embrace and to follow the truth. I do therefore again humbly beseech all the pastors and guides of the Lord's people to consider this holy rule and these worthy examples and to practice it, that the people of the Lord may be brought into true concord and brotherly harmony.

Lastly, it pertains also to rulers in civil matters to maintain this unity according to the truth. They are to minister justice and true judgment to all, to punish the evil doers and to cherish and maintain good. Mercy and love is also necessarily required in them, that they may deal as fathers when they correct and chastise. Otherwise, great mischiefs ensue, even to the disturbance of all godly peace and concord. For let a ruler, a judge, or a mighty man be void of religion, and with it given to anger, and he will be ready to beat them down and crush them in pieces. The frailties and sins are many that come from some of Christ's sheep and lambs, as there are the weak, the sick, the bruised. Therefore, lift up your hearts in earnest prayer to God that he will power down the spirit of fatherly love and mercy on rulers and judges, that they may deal with the Lord's flock with such regard as they may answer before Christ.

If we honor and embrace the truth, if we practice the rules the Lord has given us, every one performing those duties which the Lord commands, the rulers and judges, pastors and governors in the Church, as well as all private persons, we shall grow into this holy unity which the Holy Ghost here praises. And we shall receive all heavenly gifts and blessings, yes, even that great blessing of all blessings, life forevermore. Grant this unto us, O Lord, for thy dear Son's sake, our redeemer and Savior, to whom with thee and the Holy Ghost are three persons, yet one everlasting God whom we worship. To you be all honor, glory, dominion, and power, forevermore. Amen.

FINIS.

A Sermon on the Parable of the Sower[14]

To the Right Worshipful Mr. John Hutton Esquire, George Gifford wishes health and increase of worship.

It is more than half a year since I handled this Parable of the Sower in a sermon at London. As I was instantly urged by a friend which heard me to put it in writing, although I was very unwilling at the time for various considerations, yet I made some promise if time should allow. Afterward, when I would have very gladly been released of this promise, I had no means to obtain it. I have therefore at the last, as nearly as I could, set down in writing what I then preached. I know I have omitted some things in the particular applications and exhortations which I made: and I also have added some things which either then did not come to mind or I did not have time to handle. I am bold to present and dedicate this to you, as I am dutybound, not only with this common and general bond we share in that for such a long time we have professed the glorious gospel of Jesus Christ, but more especially those who are so well

---

[14] *A Sermon on the Parable of the Sower*, taken out of the 13th of Matthew. Preached at London by M. George Gifford and published at the request of various godly and well-disposed persons. (London for Tobie Cooke, dwelling at the Tigers head in Paul's Churchyard. 1582).

known to you. Seeing as I was born and brought up under you, my parents receiving benefits daily from you, I think I ought, when I am not able to repay you, at least show some token of a grateful mind. But especially I am moved with consideration for the greatest blessing which all my kindred have enjoyed from your hand now so long in providing and procuring their spiritual instruction. I pray that you will accept my good will and count me as one who prays to the Lord for you, that he will multiply and increase his good gifts still in you, to the glory of his holy name, the benefit of his Church, and your endless comfort in Jesus Christ. Amen.

Yours forever to command in the Lord,
GEORGE GIFFORD.

A Sermon upon the Parable of the Sower

"The same day went Jesus out of the house and sat by the sea side. And great multitudes were gathered together unto him, so that he went into a ship, and sat; and the whole multitude stood on the shore. And he spoke many things unto them in parables, saying, 'Behold, a sower went forth to sow. And when he sowed, some seeds fell by the wayside, and the fowls came and devoured them up: Some fell upon stony places, where they had not much earth: and forthwith they sprung up, because they had no deepness of earth. And when the sun was up, they were scorched; and because they had no root, they withered away. And some fell among thorns; and the thorns sprung up and choked them: But other fell into good ground, and brought forth fruit, some an hundredfold, some sixtyfold, some thirtyfold. Who hath ears to hear, let him hear,'" (Matt. 13:1-9).

At the time when our savior Christ came into the world, the Jews already had the word of God, the temple, and synagogues where they heard God's word read and expounded. And yet their state was very miserable, for they were as sheep without a Shepherd. Their teachers, the scribes and pharisees, being choked with covetousness and puffed up with vain glory, had grown corrupt in their customs and, in turn, had corrupted the word with their teaching which was cold and powerless. For this reason, the people had no desire to hear them. But when John the

Baptist, the forerunner of Christ, was raised up to proclaim the Gospel and to prepare the way for the Lord like a loud trumpet, the power of his word shook their hearts and roused their drowsiness. For this reason, the crowds of people in and around Galilee and Judea were hungry to hear the preaching of John the Baptist and Jesus. When Jesus himself began preaching and exercising his divine power in working wonders, there was a majesty in his person that amazed his hearers. For this reason, his fame spread far and near. The people came from all directions in droves to see and hear him. They seemed to forget themselves and their state, leaving all their worldly affairs behind. So great was their zeal that husbandmen left their ploughs and craftsmen left their crafts and followed him into the wilderness with their wives and children.

So, it seemed that the greatest part, or at least an innumerable multitude, was embracing the heavenly doctrine. But our Savior shows here that out of this great number of people that were so zealous and travelled so far, there were three groups out of four that did not profit by his teaching and were therefore still creatures under damnation. Only one group of the four were true scholars. Because we are rank hypocrites for the most part, prone to deceiving ourselves, Christ Jesus laid open the matter plainly and with such a familiar example, that unless we just willingly choose to be blind to the matter, each man should be able to see where he stands.

This example is one of a sower of corn who casts his seed abroad on the ground. Some seed falls by the

A Sermon on the Parable of the Sower

wayside, where the path is beaten smooth and hard like pavement by men's feet, and so the seed stays on top of the ground uncovered for birds to come and eat.

Some falls on rocky ground, or as Luke says, "on a rock," where there is only a thin layer of earth on top. Because the earth that covers it is extremely shallow, it springs up quickly, fresh and green, seemingly healthy enough to provide the farmer a harvest. But because the root cannot spread itself deep enough to get nourishment out of the ground, when the parching heat of the sun beams down on it, it is scorched and dies, and never brings forth any fruit.

Some seed falls among thorns, but there is no depth of earth for the seed to grow, so a stalk grows up and gets as far as the ear, before the thorns that grow up with it choke it out so that the corn in the ear cannot ripen. So, the fruit that it seems to be able to produce comes to nothing. Some other seeds fall on good ground and grow up and bring forth seasonable fruit, some as many as thirty kernels of corn, some as many as sixty, and some a hundred. This is the Parable.

Now for its meaning which we don't have to explain, for Christ himself expounds and interprets every part of it a little later in this chapter. The seed is the word of God. The sower is the preacher and publisher of the same, for as the sower fills his hand and scatters the word abroad upon the ground, he does not set it seed by seed, or choose a place for every seed.

Your hearts are the ground on which it is cast. You are the hearers and those among whom the seed is sown. The condition of your heart relates to one of these four conditions of the ground where the seed falls. And because the seed has been and is still sown among you daily, this passage of Scripture is a touchstone for each one of us to try ourselves against, to see whether we have rightly embraced the Gospel to salvation. For how careless it would be if, when we have such a just and clear rule that we don't measure ourselves by it. But going on, consider whether we are one of those three evil sorts of ground which receive the seed but bring forth no fruit, thinking we will be well if we hear and profess the Gospel after any manner.

Those who receive the seed by the wayside are those who hear the word and do not understand it. Then the evil one comes and takes it away from their heart. In these first kind of hearers, we should observe how their hearts were hard and smooth like a path that is trampled and beaten with men's feet so that the word cannot get inside but lies above exposed and uncovered. As a very hard and smooth path that is like pavement, so also through deceitfulness of sinning the devil has made the hearts of these unfit to receive the heavenly seed of the word. So then afterward, the crows and other foul follow the heels of the sower to pick up and devour the kernels of grain that lie uncovered. In much the same way, the evil one comes like a greedy foul into the assemblies where the word of God is preached to take it away from the hearts of the people that it may not grow there.

This may seem strange to some, that Satan should gain entrance among God's people, especially when they are about the best and most holy exercises of hearing the word and prayer. However strange it may seem, and however many may be so foolish to think that the devil has nothing to do with them or does not come near them when they are practicing holy worship, we are to believe Christ who tells us otherwise. We are wise to consider that when we are nearest that which should do our souls good, then is this enemy most ready to work against our spiritual growth.

If this was not uttered by our Savior Christ himself, we might wonder how so many can hear the word and yet carry away almost nothing of any purpose. Let a man tell a long tale, and his hearers have sense enough to recite it over again and to keep it in their memory a long time after. But let the preacher speak ever so plainly to those who sit and look him in the face, and if he doesn't ask of them almost as soon as they leave the church what they heard, it would be as the saying, "in one ear and out the other." They may say, "It was a good sermon," but if you were to ask what doctrine he spoke about, they would likely pause and answer, "we are not able to carry away as much as someone else, nevertheless we hope that we are as good toward God as they that carry away most." They will also confess that the word of God is good, and that we should be ruled by it.

Let us therefore dearly beloved (if we desire not to be one of these) mark well the subtle slights and policies of the devil, how he handles and conveys the matter with this kind of people. There is no doubting this. If he can, he will draw away the mind from hearing the sermon. If there is no worldly business to be done, then maybe a game of cards or tables or some other honest recreation with friends may be possible. This is the surest way, if he can attain it.

But what if he fails here? Then men come to the place where the seed will be sown and sit down, with a mind to hear. The next way to divert the seed is to come to the assembly with them, seeking how to deprive them of the word once they hear it. His best way is to put them to sleep, because they would then be as good as absent. Or maybe he can cause them to slumber, so they may hear only a sound and confused humming without any realization of what was said. Even if they hear a few sentences, they do not know the context of what was said before.

For those who may not be drowsy, he seeks to convey some thoughts into their minds to preoccupy them, and in this way he draws their attention away from what is being preached. The mind of a man is light and inconsistent; if he can get it going in one direction, it often connects to as many links as make up a whole chain, and in the meantime, the preacher goes on but the hearer is not listening to what is being said. And so, when his mind returns to listening, he will have no sound knowledge of the things that were spoken, only a confused opinion. Occasionally some word or sentence will be picked up by the mind and carried so far, so that they are preoccupied with that train of thought for some time before returning to what is being said.

Seeing this great danger, when we come to hear God's word taught, we should hold ourselves accountable that we go about it with great effort, for we are encountering Satan hand to hand, who busily seeks to steal away our heart in order to make the word fruitless in us and cause us to sin. No one hears the word rightly who allows their mind to wander. We owe the word reverence, with steadiness of mind set on it and a commitment to keep it. Herein is a lesson for every man to apply to himself when he is going to hear the word, to think, "I am now going about a great work, I shall be too weak if the Lord God does not mightily assist me. I am not to sit down at ease, but to wrestle and struggle with the devil, and with all the corruptions of my flesh and hardness of my heart, I must work to keep my mind steadfast upon the word, that I may receive it with all reverence and fear as the word of the great and glorious God. I am not to judge it of my own pleasure, but to crave wisdom from the Lord. I am not to hear it and then let it go, but I should strive to keep it as a most precious jewel locked up in my heart, that I may guide myself thereby."

We shall be more greatly moved to do this if we consider what a companion we carry about with us and what a guest we lodge with it, when we hear the word and do not keep it. For Christ tells us that it is the devil who does this. He is as a greedy foul that devours the seed that was sown in our heart. If we do not hold ourselves accountable for preventing him from possessing our minds and hardening our hearts against the word, then let us continue hearing with drowsy minds, hearing and not understanding that this is God's holy word and not the word of a man.

If you think it is a most miserable thing to have so filthy a beast and so foul a spirit lodging with you, if you think it is a most vile slavery to be vanquished and overcome by so horrible an enemy and to be lead captive by such a tyrant, then also realize how miserable a thing it is to be the kind of ground that receives the seed by the wayside. For if you see that it is no mortal man, but the Lord Jesus Christ himself who tells us that the devil is not only near, but dwells in these kind of hearers, hardening their hearts and blinding their eyes, we surely must believe it. He that deeply considers the state of our church today will soon confess that there are many of this first sort of hearers. They will know it right well by this, that they are not able to judge or put difference between sound preaching and vain prattling. They don't know when the preacher is giving forth wholesome food, and when there is nothing but chaff and wind. You may hear them highly commend a sermon, as a matter worthy to be written in letters of gold, when indeed it does not even deserve to be noted with a piece of coal. I am not speaking of these silly wretches who were never even acquainted with preaching, for that would be no great marvel. Rather, these are unable to tell the difference between chalk and cheese, or judge between colors, even though for so long they have been hearers of the word and yet are none the wiser because they are unable to determine when sound conclusions are drawn out of the word. It is all one with them, whether the reasoning is good or bad, strong or weak. They may perceive a little show of a reason, although they are never sure, and that which is so obvious and absurd that a child may laugh at seems to them a very strong pillar to lean on. When they hear preaching, it is nothing more than a glorious show of learning to them, a sweet ringing voice, about matters so strange and strangely handled that they may be brought to a state of wonderment. Satan has many chaplains fit for this work, to serve the vain humor of such people, and to set themselves up after some pompous sort, seeking their own vain glory rather than the glory of the Gospel and the conversion of souls.

The second kind of ground are those who receive the seed on hard rock, where there is some entrance, and the word has a shallow root in them, as it were in the soft *top* of their heart. There it is covered a little, and it grows up quickly, and springs fresh. They seem to be stout and excellent professors. They brag of great zeal. A man would take them to be sincere, and so they believe themselves to be. But when the sun rises high in the sky, which is to say that the fiery trials of persecution come, they stumble and fall away. And because the word had no deep root in them, it withers and brings forth no fruit. This group also are not profited by the word of grace but are still castaways and damned creatures.

In this kind of ground, or in these hearers, if we note well, we see that which is strange and wonderful when Christ testifies of them that they receive the word with joy. These are not blasphemers or persecutors of the word. They receive it with joy and take such pleasure in it that returning they can say, "Surely this was a very notable sermon and well handled. I am glad I heard it, as it does me as much good. I would walk a mile to hear it again." Is this not both miraculous and fearful, that a man may go this far and yet still be a castaway? We should not wonder when the holy scriptures give such a sentence against those traitorous villains who set themselves against God, and tread down his laws. But when God utters such a sharp sentence against this zealous kind of man, it should cause us to wonder and make us tremble. When we understand that a man may be zealous and ready to hear preaching, understand it and carry it away to let it grow in his heart and bring some joy in it, and yet still abide under the curse, we should be concerned with the true condition of our own heart.

Some will object and say that this is not a good manner of teaching, for true teaching is to build up and edify our faith, and this teaching seems to take away the certainty of the faith from all so that no man can tell whether he is saved. For by what means can a man make a better trial and proof of his faith than that he gives heed to God's word, understands it, hides it away in his heart, and finds joy in it? If such a man may be damned, who are we to not despair? I answer as Paul did in 1 Corinthians 10:12,

A Sermon on the Parable of the Sower

"He that thinks he stands, let him take heed that he does not fall." If such an admonition was necessary for the Corinthians, it is necessary for us all. One of the principal ends and uses of preaching is to give men warning so that they do not deceive themselves with every kind of faith or joy in the word, but rather look for good and sound proof in themselves which does not bring men to despair but to assurance of true godliness. This should cause them to beware lest their hearts be still hard within. This should move us to test themselves lest we are deceived by a vain shadow of a dead and fruitless faith. For Christ said, "these believe (Luke 8:13) and joy in the word, and yet are damned."

Let us now come to the application of this point, which is to see how we are to deal with ourselves. When we receive the word, take heed that we give it depth of earth enough. Do not allow your heart to be hard like a stone but allow the soil of your heart to be dug up and softened all the way to the bottom so that the word may take root deep enough. For what a miserable thing it is when Christ has given us warning so plainly, for a man to be zealous for the Gospel, not only willing to hear, but possessing an earnest desire, taking pleasure and delight when he hears, yet because he does not take heed to do according to what he hears, his hearing only further increases his damnation.

Many men think it goes well with them if they only receive this testimony from men. He who is a sound protestant takes delight in the truth. This indeed is a token that one fears God, but our chief dealing is between God and our heart, and whether or not our heart is hard and rocky. Those whose hearts are soft and affectionate toward God are a thousand times happier, because God's word takes root in them, causing them to tremble at the majesty and power of his name. Their tender heart mourns for the sinner who, to the contrary, has no conscience of sin, but who are hardened in their affections. Although they seem to be in good standing, they are cursed and miserable.

Let every man therefore that goes from the sermon, carry this with him: I hear by Christ's own words that there is a stony ground where the seed falls, where it grows some but not deep enough, it springs up but does not bring forth fruit. This is a sorrowful situation, and if I should be identified with this group, all my labor is lost that I gave to listening to sermons. I would have been much better off had I never heard one. Though I felt that I rejoiced in it, I would rather not have heard it. For Christ said that some of the reprobate hear the word with joy. So, if I do not examine my own heart, I may for all this be still damned. Therefore, I must not satisfy myself with this, but see that I cover the word deep enough, that my heart stays soft, that I feel the root go deep, yea, so deep that it can never be rooted out. And let us continually cry unto God and say, "O Lord make soft my hard and stony heart, let it be a melting heart, that thy holy word may grow in it forever."

I would to God, this doctrine of our Savior Christ, might make every one of us tremble and shake. For indeed, if it is well considered, it is such a fearful understanding that it should cause the hair of our heads to stand up. For then we would not so carelessly continue in the hardness of our hearts. There would not be so many backsliders in times of persecution. There would not be so many ready to pull in their heads at the first sign of danger or persecution. Neither would so many consider themselves to be professors that are nothing more than empty barrels which give a great sound. We must realize that hearing the word rightly requires great labor to make this stony ground soft and readied, fit to receive this heavenly seed. And he who is not careful in this point, so as to allow his heart to grow so hard that even a continual rain dropping on it cannot make it softer, nothing can make his heart relent. This may teach us then to stop being amazed when we see so many willingly desire to be taught and yet have such little remorse for their sin. May the Lord for his mercy's sake make us wise and sharp-sighted to judge ourselves, so that we are not led forward in a carnal profession, but give credit to our heavenly teacher who has opened his holy mouth to instruct us so plainly, to warn us beforehand of the great danger we face. We must stir up ourselves, and quicken our dull spirits with all humble submission, bowing down our necks to receive the doctrine of our Lord, and opening our hearts in such a way that he may dig in them and thrust in his spade to the bottom. For otherwise, it cannot go well with us. If this were practiced among us, we should not have so many hard-hearted protestants.

They need to understand the doctrine of regeneration and stand on the necessity of sincere repentance, being shown that they must be truly humbled under the burden of their sins, that they must mortify and subdue their carnal lusts. But this is too hard a crust for their old teeth. This matter robs them of their glory, and therefore they cannot willingly stand to hear it.

Let us come now to the third kind of ground, which receives the seed among the thorns. There is depth of earth enough here, so that the second sort of hearers seem to go far beyond the first and come nearer to eternal life. For here the word grows and has roots enough to spring forth for a while, and the thorns grow up with it, such that the stalk grows the ear. But it cannot ripen.

These professors do many good works and seem to bring forth the fruits of the Gospel such that wise men cannot always discern them, but think their deeds are notable. But Christ Jesus shows that their works before God are nothing but corn that cannot ripen because it is overcome with bushes. The fruit that would be produced in the ear then comes to nothing. This is a dangerous position, that a man may hear the Gospel preached, carry it away and be moved to do many good works, and yet be damned. He is a thousand-fold *mad*, therefore, who does not examine himself in this point as to what soundness there is in the fruits of his faith and how sincerely he embraces God's word.

As I said before, some would object and say this will destroy the faith, so I am sure that here it will be said much more, because this seems to take away the surest test of faith. If a man may not be able to say that "I have good works, therefore I have the true and lively faith," I answer that whoever has any good works in him, the same has faith which brings forth good works, because it is impossible without faith to do any good thing, or to have any good notion or intent. But I must also say that it is one thing to seem to do good before men, and quite another thing for it to be good indeed before God. In outward appearance there is little difference between the good deeds of them which fear God sincerely, and the untimely fruit of worldliness. But God whose eye does not look on the outward, but rather the inward affection, sees that which proceeds from faith and that which proceeds from vain glory, or some other sinister respect, and puts as great a difference between them as he did between the sacrifices of Cain and Abel. We must take heed then, that the fruits of our faith are ripe and timely, otherwise they will be good only for show and not in truth.

Let us now see what these thorns are. In Matthew they are called "the cares of this world and the deceitfulness of riches." In Luke, "the cares of riches and pleasures of this life." And indeed, these thorns grow up together with the plant. For if there were no pleasures of this life, there would be no desire for riches. Men greedily seek wealth to fill the lusts of the flesh and to pamper the body, or so they can proudly boast of achievements and ambitiously seek self-honor. For as long as a man takes pleasure in any of these, he is covetous.

What must we do then? Our hearts are as a ground that is rank and brings forth many weeds. As the prophet says in Hosea 10:12, "Plow up your fallow ground." Do not sow thorns, but rather with all diligence take care that you rid your heart of those weeds that choke out the word of God and prevent it from bringing forth fruit. So long as we allow any of these in us, to love the delicate feeding of our flesh, and to fill ourselves with pleasures, or to be gallant in the eyes of men, lifting up ourselves in our own minds, for such a time we cannot be profitable scholars in the school of Christ. We cannot offer one hand to Christ and the other to the devil. We cannot talk of the spirit and be led by the flesh. We cannot go with the gospel in our mouth and covetousness in our heart. Our works may be green before men, but they will wither before God. We will seem to be faithful when we are faithless. We will appear to be heirs of glory, while being the children of confusion. There are plenty hearers, and especially in those places where there is wealth and honor, but how many fall away because they are choked by the world? And yet we are not afraid enough of ourselves to take heed that we stand fast.

It is a great mercy of God that we have not only the doctrine laid before us, but he has also given us many fearful examples so that we may become wise at another man's expense. For when we see the world with delights and pleasures, with covetousness and ambition, are we not made of the same material they are? Yes, and we shall be overcome also, if the Lord does not see fit to have mercy on us. Hearing what Christ said, whom we ought to believe, should cause us to stir ourselves up, lest we make such a small matter out of the salvation of our souls.

When we see these thorns grow deep in our heart, we should be diligent to cut them out as fast as they spring up. We should be continually tilling and weeding this ground so that the Gospel may gain deep roots and grow up well in us. Dearly beloved, we must be persuaded of this, that though there are many godly men, they have attained this godliness with great labor and toil.

Those who think it is an easy thing to profess Christ for salvation and do little else toward their Christianity, in truth have a heart which is hard. They have thorns which will not easily be destroyed. The man who will be crowned in glory is the man who willingly gave up himself to the power of God's grace to purge his heart to make room for the holy word that it may grow there without being overshadowed and choked out by the world.

Now let us mark well what is said here, both of the stony and also of the thorny ground, how far they proceed in professing Christ and embracing his Gospel, and we shall plainly see how greatly those carnal professors of the Gospel are deceived. Faith, faith they say, this is what justifies. It is true, but not a fruitless faith. Whoever believes shall be saved is so, but not any kind of belief. For if that were the case, why would these two sorts of hearers not be saved? It is hard to imagine that when the Scripture makes it so evident and our savior Christ speaks this truth so plainly, that this gross error should possess the minds of so many. But indeed, it is a sweet doctrine, that when a man truly repents of all the lusts of the flesh, by faith he can be saved. But not until heaven and hell meet together and God and the devil are reconciled, shall these fleshly pleasure-seekers and vain proud men come to their happiness. Not until Christ denies what he has here uttered shall these be true believers.

Let men therefore take heed that they be not deceived nor be slack in examining the fruits of their faith and mortifying their vain fleshly lusts. Believe Jesus Christ, who tells you that it is not enough to hear the word and to receive it with joy and to let it grow in us. It must also bring forth reasonable and timely fruit in us.

Again, let us mark how strong and invincible an argument may be gathered from this text against all despisers of the word who are not interested in hearing. These three sorts of hearers are nearer to Christianity than those who won't hear at all, and yet they still come short. It must follow, therefore, that ignorant atheists and those who neither know nor desire to know anything above this world are very far from God. For if this matter is observed well, we would not recognize such men to be good and honest but rather dogs or swine who do not regard the precious pearl of the Gospel of God and who are ready to bark and bite at anyone who carries it with them. Let a man observe when a man is said to be a very good man, good natured, gentle, trustworthy, a man of his word, and keeps his house as well as any man in his neighborhood whether this same man is zealous for the Gospel. It does not matter that he is a quiet man and not a meddler in others' affairs. Such men are nothing more than brute beasts before God unless the Lord calls them to be zealous for his glory. Our fields are full of these, and if the Lord does not draw them to repentance, their case is most miserable. If those who were zealous for preaching and teaching and therefore flocked to hear Christ, were yet rejected because they did not believe as sincerely as they should, what can we say of those who will not step out of their doors even when they have nothing to do, unless it is to play cards or sit at tables? If such a man that is moved with some delight when he hears the word preached can be yet damned, what can we say about those hard-hearted wooden blocks of men who feel no more joy in it, then a post, when it is spoken to them? If it is possible for some to go to destruction who conform themselves and have some show of fruit by the word, where shall those wretches appear for whom the holy word of God cannot move them one whit to reform their disordered and beastly behaviors? For these hellhounds who open their mouths to reproach and slander the Gospel, I say may the Lord diminish the number of them.

The last kind of ground are those good hearers who not only receive the seed but also bring forth the fruits thereof, though not everyone alike or in the same measure. For some bring forth a hundredfold, some sixtyfold, and some thirtyfold, according to the measure of God's graces in them.

Although there are great differences in the amount of fruit each yield, they are all accepted and accounted for having good ground. These are true Christians, sincere professors of godliness. As we are taught here that it is required of all to be doers, as James said, and not hearers only (James 1:22), so are we also taught not to despise or rashly condemn those who do not bring forth as much fruit as others do. Though Christ said, "herein is my father glorified, that ye bring forth much fruit," (John 15:8), it is also true what he said in the second verse of the same chapter, "Every branch that brings forth fruit, he purges, that it may bring forth more fruit." To bring forth more fruit is most of all to be desired, that God may have the greatest glory, and yet to bring forth the least is not condemned, because in time the Lord purges those to make them more fruitful.

I do not need to stay here to continue to expound on these verses as the matter is exceedingly plain. This is the bottom of it, that all our attention in hearing and professing the Gospel should be to receive it into good ground and to bring forth the fruits thereof. Why should I stand here and rail against those who produce evil fruits and yet profess to believe the Gospel? That would be no more effective than lighting a candle in broad daylight. Not that it is not good to cry out against them, but what I have already spoken here fully discloses them.

And therefore I will here end, desiring the Lord to write these things in our hearts which we have heard with our ears, and to make us good ground that we may receive the heavenly seed and bring forth fruits of the same, that by glorifying him in this world we may be glorified of him in the world to come through Jesus Christ our Lord. Amen.

FINIS.

Other Helpful Books by George Gifford Published by Puritan Publications

Faith, Election and the Believer's Assurance
There is no greater question asked among those doubtful of their salvation than how to gain real assurance. Gifford explains this masterfully.

Resisting the Devil with a Steadfast Faith
In consideration of spiritual warfare, Gifford directs the reader to resist the devil's assaults and submit before God with the weapon of steadfast faith.

Taking Hold of Eternal Life in Christ
Is holiness of life a necessary prerequisite for getting into heaven? Do you have the power as a Christian to overcome sin? What has Jesus Christ done in enabling you to live righteously according to his commandments? How do you successfully glorify Jesus Christ in your daily walk? Gifford answers these questions to help further the eternal benefit of Christ's work in every believer.

www.ingramcontent.com/pod-product-compliance
Lightning Source LLC
Chambersburg PA
CBHW032225080426
42735CB00008B/712